To Love in spite of it all

To Love in Spite of it all

FAMILIAR TWIN SOULS STRANGERS

Iris Aguila

Copyright © 2019 Iris Aguila

All rights reserved. No part of this book may be reproduced in any form or by electronic or mechanical means, including information storage and retrieval systems, without permission in writing from the publisher, except by a reviewer who may quote brief passages in a review.

FIRST EDITION

ISBN 13: 978-1-9162146-0-6

Contents

There is a Love tale in the Sky · · · · · · · · · · · · · · · · · vii

Chapter 1	Whatever Love Is · · · · · · · · · · · · · · · · ·	1
Chapter 2	Soulmates ·	8
Chapter 3	Karmic Relationships · · · · · · · · · · · · · ·	14
Chapter 4	Home Is Where Your Heart Is · · · · · · · · ·	21
Chapter 5	It's Written in the Stars · · · · · · · · · · · ·	28
Chapter 6	The Runner, the Chaser and the Blind · · · · ·	38
Chapter 7	Obliviate ·	48
Chapter 8	Phoenix ·	56
Chapter 9	Backgammon ·	64
Chapter 10	Would You Look into the Mirror? · · · · · · · ·	71
Chapter 11	Soul Contracts · · · · · · · · · · · · · · · · · ·	81
Chapter 12	The One ·	87
Chapter 13	Destination Lost · · · · · · · · · · · · · · · · ·	101
Chapter 14	V for Vendetta · · · · · · · · · · · · · · · · · ·	107
Chapter 15	It's Time to Be Clear · · · · · · · · · · · · · ·	116
Chapter 16	Stranger's Eyes · · · · · · · · · · · · · · · · · ·	124
Chapter 17	Shadow of a Dream · · · · · · · · · · · · · · · ·	133
Chapter 18	Walkabout ·	140
Chapter 19	Unconditional Love · · · · · · · · · · · · · · · ·	148

Chapter 20	Born to Run ·	155
Chapter 21	The Eclipse ·	165
	Bibliography ·	179
	References ·	181

There is a Love tale in the Sky . . .

THERE WAS ONCE A STAR called the Sun, who did not know it was bright until someone reflected his light — the Moon. Sometimes love feels the same down on Earth as it does in the sky — always missing one another, always far from each other, never touching, our encounters ending as soon as they begin, yet this love never seems to be forgotten.

We may exist at the same time and space, share the same soul, yet you are here, and they are there. The Sun and Moon love each other so much, but they give each other space to shine. Without the Sun, the Moon will have no light, but she doesn't try to shine like him, to dim his light, because she knows her time will come.

We chase each other in a never-ending cycle, because, despite our differences, we need one another to fulfil our life's purpose. These differences get frustrating sometimes, but we balance each other out: when the Sun gets to fire up, the Moon comes in to cool things down; when it gets too dark, and hope seems lost, the Sun comes in to shine his light.

The Sun and the Moon love each other so much that they chase each day and night; it's written in the stars that they are meant to be together. So the heavens give them the chance to meet once in a while, and once they finally do catch up with one another and kiss, the whole world just stares in wonder at their eclipse.

CHAPTER 1

Whatever Love Is

I HAVE ALWAYS WONDERED WHAT brings people together, so I could not help but wonder why we are attracted to relationships that seem to be destined.

We are evolving, and so are our romantic relationships; we are no longer satisfied by those relationships that are convenient or that seem to fulfil a specific ideal that our family or society have taught us we should aspire to.

We all have ambitions – things we want to do, to achieve – but one of the greatest ideals we hold on to in our lifetime is the ideal of true love. The idea of finding *that* someone we could say is the 'one', someone who would give purpose, another meaning, better quality to our life and make us feel complete, somebody who will love us no matter what. We seek for that once-in-a-lifetime type of love, and not everyone accepts that they want or need the 'one' right away, but deep down everyone craves for such love.

In our search for the absolute, we hope to establish meaningful and deep connections with others, but sometimes we choose different paths and make compromises with ourselves in order to pursue this ideal.

Many of these routes lead us to unfulfilling relationships. However, it is these relationships that often lead us to self-development and meeting the person who is right for us. We march in all these relationships with one motive, and that is to find the one we are looking for, but, in the process, we stumble upon different people, blockages, hardships and difficult lessons that we must learn. We strive for harmony and happiness but continue to experience a certain disconnection with our partner.

The idea of finding the 'one' in modern times can be problematic when you have choice like never before. You have to trust yourself and feel certain about something that you cannot be certain about.

Sometimes we encounter powerful connections we cannot explain rationally; we simply feel pulled towards one another, and this is way beyond physical attraction, flirting and romance as we know it. There is just no logical explanation.

There is something incredibly familiar about a specific person that is unexplainable, a deep energetic connection that can't be reasoned out. We sense this person's presence, we are pulled towards them, and they are drawn towards us, yet we don't know why. When we come in contact with this type of people, we just 'know' and 'feel' they are in our lives for a good reason. We somehow know these people, and we react to them from a very basic place – our soul – and we interact with them through energy.

Though some of us may experience several karmic and *soulmate* relationships in our lifetime, those relationships do not have to be of a romantic kind; often they are with just a friend, a colleague or a family member.

Some people we meet in this life have powerful lessons for us; we are pulled towards them, but they aren't supposed to last. These partnerships come into our lives to confront us, and when they leave our lives, the relationship ends. We are transformed, and that is usually quite a difficult process.

Love is not always the fairy tale you see in the movies; the reality is much different. There are, in fact, three types of relationships, and in each one of them you will think you have found the 'one', but these relationships cannot be compared with each other; their influence and role depend on what stage we are in our own lives. And we often don't realize which type of relationship we had until long after it is over.

Our relationships reflect the energy we hold inside. What we draw into our lives is what we think and believe we deserve, what we think is right, how we feel, and we simply attract at whatever frequency we are currently vibrating on.

Karmic relationships trigger those internal issues that we do not want to deal with; they mirror ourselves and how we feel about the outside world and others. The next level, after we master those lessons is often the meeting with the soulmate.

Soulmates are those people who bring out the best in us. They are the feel-good people in our lives, they are the ones we often choose to marry and build a life with. A soulmate relationship differs from a karmic relationship in the type of lesson that is learned and how it is presented. Soulmates are the ones who care about us the most, unlike a karmic partner whose only interest is of his or her own self and needs.

However, none of those relationships put together is anything compared to the experience of being connected with our *twin flame*, the one soul that is our perfect match.

Twin flames are a combination of both karmic and soulmate relationships, which is often regarded as an urban myth. It is one of the most divine, intense and rarest experiences out there, but it isn't just someone we connect our soul energy with but also someone with whom we share the same soul. As the theory states, it is believed that twin flames were once one soul that was split into two.

Throughout their lives apart from each other, they develop as separate individuals and each becomes a whole new person. But despite that, both feel something is missing, something that was once a huge part of their lives, and struggle to comprehend what it is, so the journey to seek whatever it is that will complete the missing puzzle piece is inevitably ongoing.

However, there are a lot of misconceptions around twin flames, and even though you are subconsciously looking for your lost twin, it's not surprising if you form a passionate connection with someone else and think they are the 'one'.

Unfortunately, due to all the misinformation out there, this is very easy to do. There has been a lot of confusion since 'twin flame' became the buzzword. A decade ago, no one had even heard of this term, except perhaps the people interested in the occult.

As never before, people are investing so much into love and, strangely, as never before, are so disillusioned by it.

One of the reasons we get so confused about what kind of relationship we are in is because of all these connections and challenges they pose, none of which are about appeasing us or making our egos comfortable.

Not everyone will be lucky enough to meet his or her twin flame in this lifetime, but if we do, it will have extraordinary repercussions on the relationship, and our lives.

We all need different types of relationships at different times in our lives, and it is these connections that help us learn the meaning of real bonds. These are life lessons and experiences that we have to go through in order to find the 'one' and, eventually, find ourselves.

Not everyone is interested in finding the 'one', and that's fine, but I have to say I cannot think of anything more beautiful than waking up and having right beside you someone who adores you and wants you as much as you want them.

Very often, you don't get to experience all the layers of love, but when you do, it will make you feel so grateful. The choices you made, everything including all the drama, breakups and hurt, if it led you to this person, then it was worth walking to the ends of the earth for.

Many individuals in the spiritual community seem to use a language only some of us apparently understand to describe relationships, so much so that I think we have grown to have a slightly false idea of what love is.

If you try to understand your connection through any form of divination, you will probably find yourself hearing different replies, most of which you won't like hearing or which will not serve you and are just too narrow to describe something as limitless as love.

So if you were looking for an answer but somehow managed to get even more confused, don't forget we are talking about love – ditch the terms. Love is whatever it means to you and whatever you want to call it. And it may be something entirely different from someone else's experience; the terms used are just words attached to feelings. Drop the whole twin flame and soulmate thing altogether; love does not have twelve steps and rules to follow to unite with your other half – love is love. Even if we come from different places, believe in different gods and speak different languages, our hearts beat as one, for love has no barrier.

The fact is, only you, your twin flame and the divine are in this loop about the veracity of your relationship, and one of the most significant lessons of the twin flame journey is learning to trust your own judgement and believing what's coming through.

In life, we all start off on the side of the road we think we should be on, but the truth is that sometimes that path varies immensely from where we presumed we were. We take decisions based on our background and upbringing, never stopping to think whether we are pursuing our own heart's desires or the expectations of those closest to us.

We may have forgotten what love really is about; unconditional love doesn't play by the rules of our modern society, where those principals mainly relate to vows of loyalty, marriage, sexual attraction, family ties, where we love each other mostly because of something.

Nowadays, of course, this has become only metaphorical – a love that can conquer everything, a love with no boundaries, a love that only knows how to love, that's completely free from expectations. There is no *because*. You love for no reason and every reason.

The New Age twin flame fairy tale of a man and woman coming together in a marriage made in heaven is a throwback to medieval myths of knights and princesses.

Remember that all you have read has been translated by a human being whose ego could have been interfering with the spiritual message. In today's modern world, twin flames are here to work with our current day's situations and bring more love into this era's society.

People automatically give up thinking that it's only a fairy tale, that it's not real. But there must have been an original happening or incident, or where did the fairy tales come from in the first place?

Although twin flame connections are not about conventional romance which ends up in marriage, they are in fact triggers to make us come out of these stereotypes and look beyond. They trigger us to learn about true love, which does not have to necessarily fit into our concept of ideal romance.

Instead, see your twin flame journey as a collection of books on a shelf: as one ends, another one begins.

So when you think about the 'one', think of that person as someone you would write a story with; it probably won't be a perfect epic novel, and you'll have to slay more monsters than you ever thought you would. But something about the shared values and devotion would give you strength and hope that one day you will have your 'happily ever after'.

Everything happens for a reason; there is a tremendous correlation between thoughts and reality; I truly believe that. Pay attention to your vivid dreams, feelings; watch the patterns in your life: they are the key to unlock the mysterious doors in your lifetime and the ones you had before.

If you find yourself reading this book at this moment, the universe has brought you all this way to remind you of the wisdom you possess; others can only try, but only you can know.

The answer you are looking for is already within you; you just have to seek.

This book is about love . . .
The love you have
The love you want
The love you need and the love you seek . . .

CHAPTER 2

Soulmates

YOU MAY ALREADY KNOW WHAT a soulmate is supposed to be like; you might have even been longing for the moment that you would finally meet yours. Without any doubt, this is a relationship that will change your life– this very deep soul attraction, an instant connection right from the beginning, an uplifting feeling. There will be no judgement; you will be two equals who trust and encourage each other, think very much alike, are best of friends and offer each other a shoulder to cry on.

Usually, from the moment we meet this person we have a feeling they will play an essential role in our lives; there is an undeniable connection, as if we've known one another before. This kind of familiarity doesn't have such electrical power as a karmic relationship, but rather settled energy. Nevertheless, you will always feel a strong, energetic connection with them.

In this relationship, both of you will be on the same level, feel the same – and this is really important, because if it's not true, you might have found yourself in a karmic relationship, which is entirely different.

The name says it all – break down the word, and you can find the meaning yourself; this person is a mate for your soul, and once you you're connected to your own soul, you will attract someone who will match you on the same level. Unlike karmic relationships, a soulmate relationship is based on self-work, connecting to your own authentic self, yet unlike the karmic connection that pushes you towards that change, you are doing it from your own desire. When you do this, you will attract others who have done the same. So once you do your self-work, you will find someone who has done the same; it will be pretty special.

These beautiful types of connections don't necessarily have to be romantic. A soulmate can be your friend, a colleague, a family member, as more often than not we find out that family doesn't necessarily mean you have to share the same blood. You may never have a romantic relationship with them, but the love and connection between you will last a lifetime.

You recognise each other through the eyes; this is the first sign. You will find yourself staring into his or her eyes for more extended periods of time than into anyone else's, but, unlike a twin flame connection, there is also a need to communicate through voice and body language.

When you were young, you would have read those novels or watched those fairy-tale movies in which people would meet and fall in love instantly, without encountering any hardships. Soulmate relationships can be like that.

They have a calmer, stable connection on the lines of a brother-and-sister relationship, but this does not mean that they do not involve chemistry and passion. It can be a slow flame that lasts a lifetime, unlike the twin flame fire dynamic that can be destructive if unbalanced.

Sometimes twin flames do not have enough self-mastery to maintain a healthy partnership and thus seek solace with the next best alternative, a soulmate. Naturally, the ideal soulmate will become your life partner, and this can only work if love and compassion are the centre of everything, but no relationship is always simple and easy; it always requires equal effort.

Some of the best marriages are between soulmates – they work very harmoniously together towards their goal, have the same career aspirations and are a good team at home in raising children.

These are the relationships that can go the distance. These are the people you should marry.

Your soulmate will reflect where you are right now in your life on all levels; everything will be revealed in the partner that you choose. The most significant indicator is that they make us feel as if it's we who need work, not them, or even issues that exist within the relationship, or sometimes one can also feel like not deserving the other person.

We have many soulmates, and their purpose is all the same: they are here to provoke and assist us in our *awakening* so that our soul can evolve. Many of us wait for years obsessing about meeting a soulmate but fail to understand what we are really asking for.

Soulmates promise growth on a deep spiritual level, and these kinds of people usually come into our lives when we are ready to make a change in our lives and find love. It is in these relationships that we experience growth through what is more often a long-lasting relationship made to bring out the best in us and help us embrace our own authentic self.

It can feel amazing to have a soulmate around, but they don't always take it easy on us, and this happens only because of the familiarity we feel from the moment we come in contact with them.

In order to mature, we need a solid foundation to start from, a place that allows us to start blooming by acknowledging who we are in this minute. It is our soul-level agreement with them that will help us recognise the primitive parts of ourselves and learn where our real potential lies.

The spiritual growth process awakened from such connection includes learning about true love, being candid with ourselves and with others; it will teach us to give and receive love by replacing ego-based behaviour and thoughts with actions that come from our higher selves, sometimes in a very confrontational and even painful way.

It takes a lot of time, perseverance, dedication and learning of a lot of lessons to achieve a state of growth and balance in our life, and this happens through the challenges our soulmate energy presents us with.

A soulmate will generally be on the same path as you, meaning they have the same desires as you, regardless of their needs and wants and even their goals. A soulmate is a person whom you feel instantly comfortable with; you are both willing to grow, want to spend time together. You don't feel threatened in any way by who they are; there is a deep respect for every part of the other. You can talk to this person for hours and never get bored; you can tell them things, and they won't judge you.

But it is a false belief that soulmates are tailored to have a relationship that functions perfectly. Soulmates do split because of how powerful the connection is, and this can be overwhelming for someone who is not ready, or there may be emotional issues that hold you apart, or they just may not be your only soulmate.

Soulmate relationships are often not forever, and this is because the connection can be too intense or there is a specific karmic energy to this relationship that seems to come to a close once the necessary lesson has been learnt.

Some soulmates come into our lives with their only objective being to help us realise our greatest potential and to assist us to answer those big questions in our lives and start discovering the answers to further our transformation and process of self-awareness.

There are many distinctions, but in general it is a positive, loving and gentle experience. Although you may meet someone with whom you have a strong connection, and you are happy for a while, things may turn sour; you may want different things now, you may have children together and see a side of them that is not as you hoped or you may have just outgrown each other and decided to separate, yet they will still be relevant; they will make you go into deep self-introspection and answer those big important questions about yourself. They are an essential part of your life journey, one that may lead you to an even more strong relationship with a twin flame. But many people we get attached to and love are not twin souls but soulmates.

Far too many have never recovered from a karmic relationship, because they thought that despite all the drama, this person was their soulmate, so naturally in their minds they have made it the 'one'. This can be such a waste of time and energy, but when you are with a soulmate, all those things are never an issue.

Although karmic relationships can be beneficial as well because they add challenges to our life that help us grow, soulmates, on the other hand, inspire positive change through compassion and encouragement. In a karmic relationship, your partner's energy is too similar to your own. This similar energy creates friction and unnecessary conflict. Soulmates have an easy time calling out deep character flaws that no one else will; it's easy for them because their energy is complementary to your own.

When you ask for a soulmate, what you are really asking for is growth and development that you may not even be ready for, and not understanding this creates a block in energy called karma. And while you will be still be learning life lessons, your soulmate becomes a life partner, lending you their support and giving you a guiding hand as you navigate through your own soul journey.

If you really want to connect to a soulmate, you need to come in alignment with your own soul, discover who you are, honour yourself and begin following your heart, because when you align yourself to your true self, then you come instantly into the vibrational energy of meeting a soulmate.

When you are ready to find a soulmate, you'll attract someone who strengthens you when weak. But remember, finding a soulmate does not mean you are supposed to stay with that person forever; many soulmates do, many don't. It is essential to understand that there are so many different potential soulmates out there at this time.

If you feel it's time to move on, then probably it is; people change, so our needs change and soulmates can easily become mismatched as quickly as they become matched.

But if you find that someone with whom you want to be forever, then that's just amazing! Mate with your soul, and you will find another who'll do the same, and probably another and another.

CHAPTER 3

Karmic Relationships

Karma is all around us. It's the energy surrounding us; it's all those feelings and emotions that get stirred up by the people around us.

Karma can be described as an emotionally imbalanced history with other people or ourselves; it's simply an unlearned lesson resulting from our own actions of cause and effect.

One of the first relationships that we usually enter into is a karmic one, and it is meant to change our way of life. Many people will experience this kind of contact early in their life, and this can result in the first heartbreak or get to be a long-lasting destructive relationship, with a later attempt to save it by having children. Yet the connection is so strong that even when all the signs are shouting at you, you choose to ignore them. And if you are fine remaining at that level, you will always attract relationships that are poisonous, harmful and confusing, to say the least, that are in fact mirroring what you are portraying as you.

Love relationships are always karmic in nature, and if we were to talk about past lives, not all connections were happy ones. So, when the bond is made, you have no idea whether this is good or bad, just that you are drawn to them like a moth.

The sort of people you allow into your life are a reflection of how you feel about yourself and the world. It echoes the old sayings 'like energy attracts like energy', 'the good you do, comes back to you' and 'you get served what you served'. It just means that if there were intense emotions and unresolved issues, the ghosts of our past would come to hunt us. And in order to be able to move on, the energy between you has to rise clean.

You may be praying for a better life but may not be willing to do any inner work, or to be true to yourself or know where to begin to heal.

If you view the outside world as something that needs fixing, you'll attract relationships that need fixing, or maybe you feel like you need fixing, but rather than doing it yourself you seek out or wait for someone who will do it for you. The irony is that by doing this you'll feel the emotions more intensively than if you would have faced them on your own, and this is often what makes karma so painful.

Anything that is difficult to push through is karmic, so each relationship has something that will drive us to grow, and karma is a way of describing that growth. Karma is *that* part of the situation that you resist, and any relationship that helps you become a better person, whether you learn it gently or you go through hell, is a relationship with karma.

Imagine yourself in a crowded room; you look around and see all these people: the ones who don't spark your interest are the neutral ones; they are not your type and, therefore, have no lessons for you to learn.

Every relationship that evokes a strong emotion from you is a relationship dripping with karma, whether this is a lover, family, friend or co-worker.

The question is, which issues do you want to deal with? You pick this person, you deal with these issues; you pick that person, you deal with those issues.

We are all energetic beings, and although we can't see it with our eyes, when we interact with another, the last thing you want is to paste your energy onto someone who's going through some difficult issues, and you don't want them to paste their energy onto you either.

There is a lot of compromise in a karmic couple; they might have gone into the relationship for the wrong reasons, just settled down for each other but are not necessarily in love with each other, maybe their family arranged their marriage, or they are into it for the money or for what the other has to offer.

Some karmic couples stay married for thirty years and then wake up suddenly one day and say that they never loved each other – but they had kids together, were in a comfort zone, ended up caring for each other – but were too afraid to walk away. In this kind of relationship, you will end up cheating; infidelity is very common, and the relationship just becomes toxic and dysfunctional.

Failed marriages are often the result of a karmic connection that was confused with the more compatible connection of a soulmate, but you aren't really supposed to spend your life with your karmic partner, and if you do, both partners can end up hurt and confused. Most of the time, those people who married and divorced young married their karmic partners instead of letting them go when the time came.

When genuine love is missing, then it turns into something else. It can be addictive, and it seems that no matter how many tries we give it and no matter what we do, it just does not seem to work.

Karmic relationships come suddenly and end up suddenly when karma is resolved. They are never supposed to be lasting ones unless you like arguments, unhappiness and resentment in your everyday life. If you do not choose to incorporate happiness in your life and find out where you wish to be, then you will remain in those types of relationships or keep attracting them. These kinds of bonds are meant to turn our life upside down, to replace old things that need to be changed deep within, but they aren't meant to last; the only purpose of a karmic partnership is mutual transformation. When the process of learning is over, then we must let go and move on with our lives; the relationship ends as it has served its purpose.

Wanting a karmic relationship to work is a little bit like thinking you can be your own unique self in the presence of the most beautiful person in the world to you. The first ten minutes you may still be yourself, but by the end of the day, you will become someone else. Karma steps in as you want to give the other person more time, more love, more attention than you are willing to give yourself. Feeling excitement and rushing to stand in their presence – there is nothing wrong with that unless this excitement is higher than the one you feel for your own unique self, you forget about yourself, give up your interests and pay attention only to their needs, with them becoming the reason for your existence.

Balancing karma doesn't mean signing them over your pay cheque or giving them more than what you have. Karma is created when we become separate from *that* which governs goodwill in our lives, and it comes to show you how far off your designated path you are.

Karma is your lesson to learn; there is no way for you to avoid it or dump it on someone else; it's your issue and belongs to you. If you have karma with 'John', may he be a friend, lover or brother, whatever the issue is, it's yours to work through; John is here only to show you what the issue is. And if in return he has problems with you, then that is his work to do. If he steps out of the marriage to have an affair, he creates the karma of honesty with his feelings, the karma of loyalty with his spouse and the karma of truth with himself.

Karma can be all those disruptive emotions – anger, pain, jealousy, frustration – or it can be that uncontrollable urge to put your partner so far up there on a pedestal that they never fall, while you're in the mud, so far out there that you call it devotion, dripping out with sticky conditions. True love is not possessive, or limiting; unconditional love understands that the ego will do whatever it needs to do until it burns itself out, it does not bind or cling or force. It does not say 'I will love you if' or 'I can't live without you', because when you say so you are allowing your dysfunctional ego to create a wall that traps you, because saying you can't live or be without someone shrinks the infinite love space into fear, the fear of losing the one you love so dearly. The bigger the fear, the more prominent the wall and the harder to get out, and all this because you allow your ego to make a choice for you. Let go of the fear of not being with someone, and you will discover that you will still be loved and love them whether you are with them or not.

It's not about them; it's all about you because it's your karma, your lesson, your healing; it is your ego that makes the other person responsible for your happiness.

In a healthy relationship, partners help each other discover who they are, how they need to grow, and support each other while doing it. Good karma should mean equality, giving to yourself as much as you give to them and seeing eye to eye.

It is rare for a karmic connection to make anyone truly happy; the whole time this relationship is happening, you know deep down this is hard to keep up with, and it's not going anywhere. This underlying thought is what will eventually rule it out. You ask yourself time and again, 'Do I really love them? Are they really the "One"?'

I wouldn't want you to get the wrong idea though, that karmic relationships are a bad thing; they can be incredibly passionate and give you some of the most beautiful moments of your life.

But for someone over forty, clearly, it isn't a matter of needing to mature. When they are secretly thrilled as their partner explodes in jealousy because it helps disguise all the shallow in the relationship, all the holes, it makes their ego feel that they are needed after all and, therefore, loved. Sometimes there are means to remedy the circumstance unless the decision is reached that the ultimate cure for such maladies must be used – separation. Either both of you are in a position to work through your issues with each other or you divorce. If one of you wants to end the relationship more than stay in it, there will usually be a way out that starts to develop in most cases. Carefully consider your choices and execute them, because when you make a decision, the universe conspires to make it occur.

If you can see what is broken, then you can find a way to heal it; your healing is an action done by you, for you; another person can only support you. They, however, cannot do it for you; it's your karma, your own invention done by your own design. Therefore, it is yours to heal.

Karmic relationships can be a healthy part of a beautiful life; they cause problems only when they drag on for far too long. Recognising the patterns in your dating life will help you learn from your relationships.

By following the karmic path, learning the value of personal identity and integrity and practising boundaries, our passionate expressions are given permission to flourish. From this place, safety nets are created to allow the relationship to learn through failure, through a safe environment to express your needs while having the support of your partner. By failing, we learn what is right and the path that keeps us in truth, even at times when you feel as though karma is putting you through hell, when in fact this divine path was created from absolute love.

Karma can end up in love as well when both of you are able to see and speak out loud to each other about space, that space being time together and time apart. If you see it as something that will nurture the relationship and whatever bad feelings you might have had, you would have processed them by the time you get back together or decide to part ways.

You should never have to earn love and affection from your partner; you are not in their possession. There is at least one soulmate for each one of us out there, and if you are extremely fortunate, you may even discover your twin flame.

CHAPTER 4

Home Is Where Your Heart Is

IT ALL BEGINS WITH THE sound of silence. There is no mistaking it; you don't have to go anywhere else anymore because you're at the right place, at the right time, in the warm arms of the right person: that's why it felt so wonderful when your twin flame finally hugged you.

> *And so, when a person meets the half that is his very own, whatever his orientation, whether it's to young men or not, then something wonderful happens: the two are struck from their senses by love, by a sense of belonging to one another, and by desire, and they don't want to be separated from one another, not even for a moment.*
>
> —*RICHARD H. (2004), PLATO'S SYMPOSIUM*

You cannot shake off the urge to run to your twin and hug them; they make you feel at home. Your whole body is relaxed; now you know everything will be okay. All the worries have disappeared, the weight has been lifted off your shoulders; your feet get numb and refuse to carry you anymore because they are finally home.

You want to hold your twin and never separate your bodies, you disappear into their hugs; the energy between you two is indisputable, and even people around you notice it.

The moment they clasp your hand, a nervous feeling invades you, like the one you get when you meet someone you really like, only they are not just anyone.

With every touch or move they make, that feeling is there; your heart flutters with butterflies because both of your hearts just throbbed for each other for the very first time, and you thought your heart would jump out of your chest to meet theirs.

Love is literally pulsating between you, unbelievable, yes, so intense and surreal like the sweetest dream, but yet so undeniably real.

Throughout life, we meet 'one' person who is unlike any other.

If you know who this stranger is, then you probably always have known, they have always had your heart, and you have always had theirs. There is no doubt about your feelings for them, and you know they feel the same way, without having to say a word.

Love is in the air, even when you are out, sitting across from each other, not touching at all; the energy around you is so intense that you could cut it with a knife. Also, people who are sitting around you feel it as well; they feel energised by your passion, and they wish they could have this love as well.

This connection is truly 'written in the stars'.

Their voice or laughter can trigger a familiar feeling of remembrance, and there is no need to watch them or talk to them to figure out what they want. You take one look into your twin's eyes, and you know exactly what's going on inside them, their wants and needs, their worries; you are two open books to one another, and this develops without you even thinking about it.

The eyes are the window to the soul.

—William S. (2013), *William Shakespeare's Poems And Quotes*

The eyes are the most sincere part of our body that we don't have any control over; we see someone, and with one look we send a message worth a thousand words.

It is said at the time you meet, your eyes will stop and stare, and every inch of you will point towards this stranger like an arrow ready to be shot, and with that, you've just found out that love at first sight is real.

Gazing into the eyes of the 'one' can trigger a powerful feeling of soul recognition and can be very intense; your breath gets shorter, and your heart just skips a beat, not necessarily because you are looking into their eyes, the eyes of the 'one', but because you are looking into the mirror of your own soul.

When your eyes meet, sometimes you become lost for hours on end, staring straight into each other's souls.

No matter how lost or sad you feel, one smile from them can take it all away; even just looking deep into each other's eyes will make you feel something. Lighting up every sense in you and opening your heart to theirs, being able to see straight through you, your every expression, they are able to read you like a book.

There is much more to it than meets the eye, much more happening than your heart can grasp, or your mind can understand.

The eyes are the most powerful part of the body that reveal one's emotions and feelings, and it's quite normal for couples in love to constantly gaze into each other's eyes with love and appreciation. However, when you look into your twin flame's eyes, there is something different, rather special, which holds a more profound feeling.

The emotion you feel in the presence of your twin flame will be indescribable; there are just no words that can be used to express this kind of love. It is magnetising energy that emerges when the two halves of a soul look into each other.

The eyes are the most significant tool twin flames can use to connect at a higher level; it is through the eyes that you are able to show each other what's really going on inside of your soul – not only the love, joy, happiness and appreciation but also the pain, sadness and rage inside of you. Just staring into each other's eyes will suppress the bitterness and anger within you.

The eyes form an infinite bond between the heart and the soul.

You will know what they want to say without any words coming out of their mouths; you will know what they are going through, if they had a bad day or not – you just know without them even telling you. You have this uncanny ability to know what is going on inside them even when they have not shared this information with you.

Eye contact can be a sure sign of a twin flame connection; looking into the eyes of the 'one' who was destined for you will sure awaken some deep feelings in you. Don't think you're crazy; you might feel their presence even when they're not physically there. You may feel their eyes on you even when you're alone in a room.

As small as the eyes are, they are as powerful as can be and as mysterious as the dark side of the moon. It's magical, and you won't even know what hit you; this love is fierce, and it burns hot.

If you are lucky enough to meet your twin flame, one of the most beautiful moments of your life is when they first kiss you.

You most probably already feel charmed being in their presence, drawing you to taste their lips, so the moment your lips touch, your souls are ignited, a direct bond is made from your heart chakra to their heart chakra, with an energy overdrive that runs through both your energy systems.

Describing it can be very difficult because your lips are touching indeed at a physical level, but the kiss can be felt at a spiritual level as well; that is why the twin flame kiss is so intense – it's far more complex than any other connection you ever felt in a relationship.

In normal relationships, you would connect to somebody first from the mind, from the lower chakra levels, so it's a pleasure of the flesh, an attraction, a chemical reaction. But in the twin flame connection, it is the other way round; you may not even feel any physical attraction to start with. It will be a spiritual and soul connection, with everything in reverse; the sexual attraction might come last.

But, as expected, it will be nothing like you have experienced before; it feels more magnetising and energising than traditional lovemaking, and it can lead to something called astral sex, where your etheric body, the soul, surfaces from your body for an 'out of this world' experience.

In a romantic twin flame union, the physical attraction and passion can be strong, the lovemaking can be incredibly intense, especially if you are more spiritually awakened and focused on the heart level. Intimacy will come instinctively even if you have never given yourself to someone this easily; you will give yourself entirely to your twin flame love without hesitation.

Everything stops, and it's amazing; it can easily be described as being an out-of-this-world, life-changing experience that is outside of time and the ordinary. Their kiss leaves you breathless; your mind shuts off from your surroundings, and a warm tingling sensation fills your whole body, taking you away to the castle where dreams are made.

Your energies entwine in a kind of spiritual dance, your auras stretch and amplify in a rush higher consciousness.

The feeling when you are together in this eternal moment that's outside of time and space is beyond explanation. It is the biggest, most unshakable thing you've ever felt towards another person, to the point that you get dizzy. You will know they are the 'one'; it will be like nothing else you have experienced, and each time it happens, it will give you a better picture of how your twin is on the inside.

The whole body tingling and filled with light and warmth draws everything you've ever felt with other human beings.

Of course, you connect in other relationships spiritually, but none can be compared to your twin, where the bond is made on so many levels.

Some kisses are different from others; some are better, much more intense than others and have less to do with technique or physical attraction.

The first kiss will be the most intense, of course; that's just the way life is. It's the very energy that has bound your destiny together since its inception.

You can't really know what a twin flame connection is like unless you have felt it; it isn't something easy to describe. You just know deep inside they are yours; that they are meant for you and no one else in the world. No doubt, no fear, only certainty like you have never been more sure about anything else in your life.

You don't feel like you've just met a stranger; you feel like you've known them forever but just haven't seen them for some time. Something inside you recognises them way before your mind can fully comprehend it.

Not everyone will be lucky enough to meet their twin in this lifetime, but if it does occur it will have extraordinary repercussions for the relationship and both their lives.

This joining of lips, this kiss, represents the beginning of a journey and the first steps you take that guide you towards the eclipse.

CHAPTER 5

It's Written in the Stars

*I seem to have loved you in numberless forms, numberless times
. . . in life after life, in age after age, forever.*

—Rabindranath Tagore (2005), 'Selected Poems'

SOME OF THIS IS A legend, but at least this much is a fact.

Though proof that twin flames are not a myth does not exist, the story of the 'eternal lovers' has actually been around since the beginning of time.

In Greek mythology, it is said that a long time ago we were once one with our twins; the gods created humans with four arms and four legs, but once they realized how powerful they could be together, Zeus separated them into two, male and female, letting them spend long years of their lives in searching for each other.

An oft-told tale is the one about Adam and Eve, who were made from the same flesh, banished from the Garden of Eden, who went to live on Earth but could not remember any more who they were, and wan-dered the earth apart from each other for many long years.

Yin and yang, an integral Chinese symbol for thousands of years, two opposite but complementary forces, like night and day, so different yet impossible to have one without the other, never separate, together create a totality, a complete whole. Not all things, of course, are black and white in life, but I think it's a perfect analogy for twin flame love.

Sounds familiar? Same story, different names.

Although the idea of twin souls is not a new one, it is still a great mystery to many. The term 'twin souls' or 'flames' has often been confused with soulmates, which is distinctly different.

There are usually signs and meaningful synchronicities that lead up to the meeting or reunion of twin flames, often guiding you to one another and becoming more frequent during periods of high importance when the energy shifts within the union.

There won't be signs like those you see in the movies where something magically falls out of the sky, but there will be signs. Some believe these signs and synchronicities mean something, others don't; some just think they must be mere coincidence.

There will be no magazine quiz to tell you if they are the 'one', no course or certain rules to follow because this connection does not fit in any regular pattern; you simply cannot classify it.

While it is different from the usual type of love, those characteristics aren't set in stone because everyone's experience is unique.

So many people get upset because of the articles and what other people have said about twin flames, detailing the stages of the journey as if it's a universal one-size-fits-all phenomenon.

There are a number of things that can happen; some of them might even occur with other soul connections, like the telepathic abilities.

There can be similarities, as you may have lived many lives and bonded with many people.

And the truth is that even though it's very difficult to know, I believe that the universe will give you a very unique and specific sign to let you know that somebody is your twin flame. And you won't have to go by these generic twin flame signs that can actually be as convincing as every strong soul connection.

There have been stories that one or both twins have had dreams before meeting, and those dreams felt real, like something big is about to happen. It's like your whole being is ready to meet them, and your subconscious mind knows that they're coming. It will be so crazy and irrational that you won't be able to stop yourself from beginning to believe that there's, really, a higher power involved in this.

If you want to climb a mountain begin at the top.

—Zen Proverb

But before the meeting takes place, you will learn a valuable life lesson. When you find your twin flame, you are literally trying to fit, blindfolded, two pieces of a puzzle, and it takes a few tries before you do it right, as now you rely on instinct. You have to learn to feel first and then ignition will happen.

A feeling that something is brewing – you know something is happening behind the scenes before you meet them, but you have no clue what it is or why you feel this way as the universe brews you the karmic tea of awakening with a special note at the end. Awakening is like pouring water in your teacup after you finish making your tea, and the leaves start to get stirred up. This is *ascension*, awakening.

You start feeling more and more anxious and nervous as the energy builds up like something is about to explode, and the moment you encounter this, your brewing water for the universal tea has reached boiling point, bubbling and jumping off the stove, whistling, strange, unusual sparks flying from beneath and within your being, like something is about to erupt, and you can't move a finger to stop this from catching fire.

But the moment you encounter them, you just know they are there, and they are the 'one', a simple yet accurate way of describing this feeling. Everything calms down as they set aside the hot boiling kettle, as your rational mind stops to figure out what just happened. Their eyes may not recognise you, but the soul recognition would be instant.

Standing in the presence of your twin, meeting them for the very first time, can be one of the most wonderful feelings you will ever have. The first physical encounter will be powerful, and it can trigger recognition, some call it déjà vu, either from this life or, if you believe in it, from a past life.

Everything will just click, and you've entered the love bubble phase that rapidly follows the meeting, which is usually love at first sight. This has to be felt by both of you; if it's one sided, then it's just obsession.

Looking into their eyes will remind you of the moments you two have lived, every detail that made you crazy, every sweet thing you can remember; all of this will ignite the lost feeling of love.

As the stars align, once you awaken to the fact that they are your twin soul, your buck just stops there; your quest to find the love of your life has ended. Yet, strangely, there will be a certain period in the initial stages of awakening when twin flames keep doubting if they are twin souls indeed.

Lovers don't finally meet somewhere. They're in each other all along.

—Jalal A. D. R. (2006), Rumi: Poems

Even remotely apart from each other, twins are often able to sense one another vibrationally; they are able to sense the mood of the other, and often times know what state of mind their twin is in at a particular time. Twin souls can sometimes sense when the other is ill or injured, sometimes even physically feeling the same symptoms in their own body.

Twin flames can often relate to having experienced similar life events around the same time or may have the same emotional issues or karmic energies that need to be healed together, balanced in their lives or resolved with the people close to them.

Your intuition gets heightened when you meet your twin; this may or may not involve telepathy and one or more of the 'clair' senses (clairvoyance – to see, clairaudience – to hear, clairsentience – to feel, claircognisance – to know); everyone's experience is unique. Physical contact can increase your aura energy but will not float on a cloud of intuitive skills all the time.

A twin flame soul can sometimes feel what the other is feeling, thinking or doing; the longer and deeper the bond, the more in tune they will be with one another.

You can have an actual experience of what your twin is doing or eating; you can feel that in your energy field, even if it's something you have never done, including if they are in any pain. Your senses might go wild; everything looks sharper, your hearing is acute; it is like you have supersenses.

You can feel the energy every time there is any type of interaction, even physically feel the sensation on your skin, but you may have no clue what this weird chemistry is, awkward body hormones or even the beginning of an illness.

If kundalini energy is awakened, you connect even more deeply with your twin flame and feel the intensity of love emerging. This has a massive effect on the heart, as the soul and the spirit communicate through the heart, which is the main area where the soul whispers from – it's the speaker box of the soul.

Twin flames also share the same chakra system, have the uncanny ability to absorb one another's pain or emotions and feelings that are negative, and dissolve them on the other's behalf, often before the other even feels it.

Because twins are natural empaths and are sensitive to spiritual energy, their psychic abilities can start manifesting for the first time or become more enhanced after their meeting. They can also uncover the ability to heal each other on an energetic level. Some twin souls might even resemble each other in some way or even share one or more distinct physical attributes.

As you spend more time with your twin, you will feel more energy; it will feel as if you can conquer the entire world. You may have sleepless nights in the beginning because you just aren't tired enough to fall asleep. Your twin gives you the energy to become, do and accomplish whatever you want in your life. It's just like magic; it makes everything beautifully coloured into magical emotions. It's the type of energy that could help you win a marathon, even though you haven't run since you were a little kid. It's the energy that can help you finish all your projects on time and the energy that causes you to dedicate time to your twin flame, even though you have been working all day.

There may be other mysterious similarities in each twin's day, such as messaging and calling each other at the same time, discovering that they have had the same type of meal on the same day or even had the same dreams on the same nights.

It can happen that you can see and feel within the other person, the other part of your soul you connect with; you can experience and see past lives that you have lived and experienced with them. As your clair-senses are awakened, you might be even able to see your twin's face shift physically, their facial characteristics changing to another time that they lived in at the same time as you. You can sometimes see past life aspects in them, in their character, face, body and personality. You look into their eyes, and you can see your future.

The twin flame dynamic can be overwhelming and confusing at times; the extreme highs and lows that can accompany these connections can often make one feel as if one is going crazy. This relationship most times doesn't make sense to other people and even to the twin souls themselves. The real world might just not make sense to you anymore.

Our self-defence mechanism often causes us more problems in the physical plane as our energy centre is trying to adapt to the new status quo.

And, of course, it does not help that you can't explain any of this to any of your friends or family because, try as they may, they cannot understand.

There might be odd similarities, like sharing the same dreams with your twin. Some twin flames on their journey to ascension can be brought by a common mystical dream to initiation chambers where they will be faced with their own fears and emotions. A seed seems to live within you, closed in a mysterious chamber, a living memory of an enigmatic doorway that leads twin flames into their original state of creation, where they were 'one' before their separation. The ones who follow this path are known as the 'carriers of the flame' or twin flames. To open this doorway, you must become, above all, lovers of love with a capital 'L'.

The vision takes place in virtual reality, simulating whatever you need to overcome; such chambers seem to lie under the Sphinx by the Pyramid of Giza.

Your present-day reality is, in the same way, a virtual reality, here to help you break through the walls that are still obstructing you from being who you truly are on a soul level, and expressing yourself as such in the physical reality.

After the actual meeting takes place on a physical level, the dreams and visions may suddenly diminish or seem to disappear, but that is only an illusion. You are always spiritually connected, your bond is unbreakable, and after years of separation, at key points in the reunion you are still be able to communicate.

We have faith, but sometimes we start losing it, and we begin looking for an actual sign.

When comparing your birth/natal charts some interesting correspondences and powerful aspects can usually be found; the twin flame master numbers may appear; eleven is one of the initial sequence numbers that seems to show up just at the right time in dual or triple synchronicities, 11:11 or 1:11, but unless you pay attention, you will miss those signs.

And at some point, you will think back at all the fortunate coincidences that led you to meet your twin flame. You will start to notice number patterns like 11:11 on the clock, and then, later on, 2:22, which is the relationship number; 4:44, which is the angelic presence number; and 5:55, which is the number for new beginnings. But 11:11 is the wake-up call.

You will just glimpse at the clock for no reason, and it will say 11:11, right then, right at the very moment you glanced at it. Nothing is a coincidence; it's trying to tell you something.

It is interesting to see sequences of numbers holding a close relationship with the twin flame connection. The Fibonacci or golden ratio has origins going back to 450 BC, and it begins with 0, 1, 1, 2, 3, 5, 8, 13, 21, 34, 55, 89, 144 . . . 610, 987, 1597 . . .

It might seem complicated, but what happens is actually simple. The first two Fibonacci numbers are 0 and 1, and each subsequent number is the sum of the previous two.

This is the most well-known evidence for a designed universe as it is related to everything around us from nature, growing flowers, the regeneration of skin cells, Da Vinci art and Beethoven. If the sequence begins any other way, it will not relate to the golden ratio anymore.

As 5 is to 8 so is 8 to 13, practically,
and as 8 is to 13, so is 13 to 21 almost.

—JOHANNES K. (2005), KEPLER'S ASTRONOMIA NOVA

These sequence numbers tell us a story about twin flames, from the inside, working with the building blocks of our universe, as at the beginning there was nothing, zero, no creation, just the source – God. So he created 1 and 1, the twins, and from these two numbers the rest of the sequence began, and all creation sprung.

There may or may not be magical synchronicities that are obvious signs, which can also involve numbers, such as important personal dates in each twin's life: it could be a birthday or just a date of an important event which took place in their life.

Other signs can be songs, photos or people who are trying to guide you on the right path; if you see lots of signs on the same theme, then you are receiving them for a reason, and they will continue to get your attention and appear to even chase you until you understand the message they are trying to send. You might be thinking in your mind about something and might hear the exact word or phrase vocalized. You will see messages around you like they have been personalised just for you, from TV shows to songs, movies, billboards or a conversation, which will answer your query.

But if you haven't seen any signs in a while, don't chase them; it means you are on the right path, heading in the right direction. The signs are your road map, your GPS that will guide you through your journey to the *union*.

Twin flames will often experience similar trials at similar times before and after meeting, as each soul reflects each other's lesson.

When the universe wants to send you a message, it won't bother just to show it to you on the clock; you won't miss it if it's something you need to see; it will be powerful and meaningful. Usually, it will be an event of high importance taking place at a specific date that means something to you. And the red flags will chase you until you no longer need guidance, and you're on the right path, and then they'll disappear until you require guidance again.

The typical mistake people make is misreading the signs because in reality the signs only guide them in the right direction; they do not confirm or deny anything.

They are clues you need in order to keep moving forward; a massive mistake could be to ignore what those signs are telling you. They are patterns and directions laid out in front of you, as a blueprint by your higher self, to the way back to the eclipse.

When you meet the other half of your soul, you will just know they are the 'one', because an instinctive reflex of knowing would arise and not because you verified the above signs objectively.

CHAPTER 6

The Runner, the Chaser and the Blind

THE PASSION BETWEEN YOU IS undeniable, but there is an equal amount of worry and uncertainty. You're asking a lot of questions – whether this is really love, or indeed what you want for your life.

The feeling you have right now, in the presence of your twin flame, has been suppressed for far too long. It is now coming out, and it's totally fine that you aren't able to control it, or sometimes even understand it. This feeling of love that is right now inside your chest makes you cry from happiness.

Because we are just so used to controlling and thinking our emotions through, now it seems like we have no legal right to choose when we are overwhelmed with these emotions.

Twin flame souls will feel a powerful and deep connection to one another early on. This connection is often instantaneous, although sometimes it can occur gradually over time. Either way, there is definitely no doubt that there is a powerful and unique energetic connection between them that can't be explained in words most of the time.

Yes, you never felt this way before, but this feeling may not translate into being 'in love', doesn't necessarily have anything to do with the roman-tic love as we know it; it is an unnatural love that exists more at a soul level.

Many twin flames have even crossed paths at one time or another in the past, without even realising it, and unfortunately, sometimes we miss those opportunities because we aren't ready to embrace such rapid growth.

For a start, there will be signs, and plenty of them, but you don't notice them until you have been awakened to them, and awakening actually starts with meeting your twin flame. You start becoming more spiritually aware, but it's usually only one of you, the awakened twin that can see those signs. The other, 'blind' twin is usually blissfully unaware of this until it's brought to their attention, and they will tend to 'run' from this connection.

When you meet your twin, you are usually pulled towards a volatile relationship that often moves the ground below your feet, and are magnetically drawn to the other person. You feel a powerful mix of excitement and fear, uncertainty and certainty, drifting between the need to attach and detach, as these kinds of connections move you powerfully and stir your subconscious, your shadows and everything that was hidden.

You may think that meeting your twin flame couldn't have happened at a worse time, but that is when it often occurs. This confronts your integrity and values and causes you to question what you have always known.

> *Soulmates aren't the ones who make you happiest, no. They're instead the ones who make you feel the most. Burning edges and scars and stars. Old pains and pangs, captivation and beauty. Strain and shadows and worry and yearning. Sweetness and madness and dreamlike surrender. They hurl you into the abyss. They taste like hope.*
>
> —Victoria Erickson (2017), Edge of Wonder

Twin flames always oscillate between being together and being apart, and while one plays the role of the runner, the other is the chaser, which creates an electrical instability in the union. Nevertheless, both twins are drawn to each other over and over again over time in general, because the pull towards union is so powerful, and to forget about each other goes beyond the bounds of possibility.

The push-pull, runner-chaser dynamic can happen or not; it's true that one or both of you may choose to run from the experience, and if it happens, it can feel very devastating. It's just a normal human reaction to a very intense experience, as we tend to run from confusion; this happens in all kinds of relationships all the time.

Anyone who searches the internet about twin flames will find that there is a stage quite well documented, called the 'twin flame runner' or 'separation', and not every set of twins goes through this.

For example, if ten people were given a riddle to solve, there is a significant chance that all ten solutions will not be similar; the same is true with the twin flame runner stage.

You may not have to separate from your twin, but most do. During separation, you might have periods of deep soul depression and pain that are going to drive you mad because you cannot rid yourself in any way of this connection with your twin. This feels like an obsession; in fact, the name most commonly used for this is 'twin flame obsession', and it makes you feel like a maniac because you just can't let it go, no matter what you do.

The twin who is more aware of the connection, and who is most of the times the chaser, initiates this process of wanting to get closer, but the one on the receiving end might get triggered into taking a step back because they are not aware of what is going on.

Love is a subjective notion, and the universe brews a completely different story for each one of us.

Every experience is unique, but generally, the male or the twin with more masculine energy tends to be the runner.

The chaser knows that this is to come, he feels the calling towards the eclipse and cannot wait for the exciting journey ahead. Chasers tend to be more spiritually aware in general; they identify their twin flame and want the journey to begin, to ascend with their twin flame towards enlightenment and, ultimately, unite on the astral plane.

The twin flame runner, on the other hand, knows that this is what you want; they feel something as well, which they might not know on an intellectual level, but their soul knows it. The difference is that instead of getting excited about embarking on a new journey, they fear the loss of their old self.

After all, they are being asked to drop their old life to begin a new one with their chaser, which is a lot to ask.

Runners are often too scared to confront their feelings and vulnerabilities while chasers are playing relentlessly without a safety net.

The blind twin will try to run from the feeling; depending on the person, they will try to bury themselves in work, perhaps drugs or alcohol, or they will busy themselves as much as they can to avoid the pain. Or they understand the importance of it and the challenges that lie within it, that it is a forever relationship – and that is scary. But nothing will work, and they will eventually return to the awakened or 'stayer' twin.

No matter how coherent and logical you naturally are, you will suddenly feel off balance, finding it hard to act rationally. You might frequently find yourself being highly emotional and impulsive. This is because the part of your soul which was once lost is found and needs to be unified, so that you can become whole again and heal the parts of you that have needed your attention for so long.

Runners love excuses as they sound reasonable, but in reality, they use them out of fear. There is a significant age difference, or you are at different stages in life. The runner may already have a partner and may run because they cannot do the difficult thing due to fear of upheaval. Or they are about to start a job halfway across the country; this is one of many other reasons that prevent twins from embarking on a spiritual journey, and unfortunately, many twin flames find themselves in this situation.

The runner can run for a few reasons, but primary amongst those is that they don't believe in the concept or aren't spiritually open to it. It must scare you that after all they are experiencing, all these life-changing situations, they still don't fully understand or believe in the whole process.

Being spiritually opened means more than paying attention at church and to other religious beliefs; many of us are brought up with certain views, taught in school, but until we experience those particular emotions ourselves, it can be a little bit difficult to believe.

Your twin might not have and share the same spiritual beliefs as you have; they may not necessarily believe in the whole concept of twin souls or might not even have any spiritual beliefs at all, to begin with. Being presented with these spiritual beliefs in such an intense way might be what sends them running in the first place.

When separation occurs, it can be one of the hardest things to go through, because in a way even if your twin is still present in your life, it feels more like death, like something just died inside of you. It's not about losing the love of their personality, who they are as a person in this lifetime; that is only a tiny little bit of their nature that you are experiencing. It's the whole spiritual and soul connection that you feel dying.

Trauma is caused by the soul having a part of itself torn out; it manifests as heartbreak because that is how we process the deep spiritual pain that this causes us. And the runner experiences soul shock to the same extent the chaser does.

The pain is shared over the silver cord connection that links them both, so they both feel that pain. The runner also knows that it is because of their own doing they inflicted the wound on themselves, both their pain and their chaser's.

During the twin flame separation stage, each twin takes on a role, but that role is not definite. They keep switching between roles, both equally important and painful. But neither of them gets the easy end of the deal.

First, a feeling of emptiness surrounds us because when we are separate from our twin, we literally feel as if we have lost a piece of ourselves, as if a piece of our being has been torn out, and we are left with phantom pain where it used to be. There is a feeling of burning agony, of being utterly torn apart inside as if by a real snake, till we can no longer handle the floods of vibrations in our chakras. Some people can even experience physical illness, depression, lethargy, nausea, or migraines. All these can be symptoms of twin flame separation sickness.

The chaser seems to have a wealth of resources to help them with the soul shock, whereas the runner experiences the loss differently. They are almost caught entirely off guard. Lacking the spiritual character of the chaser, the runner is more often dumped on their own to deal with these feelings, feelings they are entirely unaware of and that they don't understand.

The whole separation stage of the twin flame relationship is strange and alien to the twin flame runner.

They have never felt this way before, this intense level of pain and despair, and don't understand what is happening, why it is happening or how to stop it.

Once they do reach the realisation and the truth of the twin flame relationship, they quickly end the runner-chaser stage. Their actions may not make sense to us, and it may feel to us like they are the cause of our pain, but in reality, they are just scared, confused and struggling to come to terms with a new understanding.

The pain and fear drives the chaser to pursue their twin. The fear of never being happy or never finding love without their twin soul can be very tormenting to cope with. All those feelings of betrayal and abandonment beset the chaser, but the runner does not have an easy time either.

The runner feels the same shock and pain, the same fear of their soul not being whole, but they often don't understand very easily why they feel this way. Their thinking shifts as they come to terms with the things that they had trouble denying, the ebb and flow, and they don't know what to do about it.

Recognition and soul shock is where twin flames recognise each other on the soul level, and all the hurt and negativity from past lives come to the surface for clearing. And there is so much energy coming up at that encounter, that sometimes we cannot handle that energy.

There could be a disruption at this point to the process, and you will experience a mild separation for a while, depending on the circumstances, but when you get back together again, you will experience the connection like nothing else you have ever known. The depth of this connection will lead to you and your twin confronting the most obvious of differences that need to be ironed out before a union is possible.

Twin flames are the masculine and feminine energy charge of one soul, being of the same frequency, and they now start to kindle for the very first time. There is a period that can last between weeks or months up to a year, but generally not longer than that, when twins connect at the pure frequency of the soul, without the interference of the brain. You probably never have felt this peace before — as if even if you died at that moment, it wouldn't have felt better — because it is such a state of bliss and tranquillity, almost indescribable like nothing could ever match it, but then that frequency will start to drop, which it is supposed to because we are here to live in the physical world.

What you are doing as a twin flame when you are in that period of time, is that you are at your optimal frequency; you are actually being the real you.

This period is vital, as it changes the whole energy of the twins, their lives, the template, the entire perception of love and of connection, on what they thought relationships were, which is all blown out of the water. Everything is in reverse, the whole paradigm of love, and the more the twins experience it, the better.

When they leave, it's heart breaking, an intense soul shock as you feel them ripping your soul into two. There is a hollow feeling of emptiness, when the void deep down your soul is not filled.

This soul shock, as painful as it is, is what will eventually bring them back together. Soul shock is not just a side effect of the runner-chaser stage but also an essential part of ending it. Without it, the runner would just keep running; they would not stop to think and consider a new perspective. As cruel as it sounds, nothing helps the runner better to see the reality of the twin flame relationship than the actual pain that comes from denying it.

Sometimes a runner runs because they are being asked to work on themselves before they have accepted that this is needed. But all it takes for them is to learn the truth and believe it. So when they finally get the opportunity to get what they want, if they suddenly start running from it, then they have fallen victim to the same cycle and fears.

When the initial chaser is now a person who has healed their abandon-ment issues and are no longer in the needy space, what happens is that the initial runner becomes attracted to the initial chaser. But the paradox is that now the initial chaser realises they don't need the runner anymore, so they switch. The person who was the initial chaser takes a look at their twin and recognises all the shadow aspects that they have been working on to heal in themselves, unhealed in their twin. And chances are they are not going to stick around while their twin is dealing with that, so they become the runner.

You, being the chaser in most cases, need to learn and shift your thinking and refrain from judgement, assumption and blaming them and expecting them to fix themselves without you doing the same. For this is a two-way street— whatever you do and think, they most likely are doing the same and are as conflicted as you are.

The fact is, they would not run if they were ready for the twin flame relationship.

The runner might stop running only to discover that the chaser has turned into a runner themselves, and to understand why this can happen you need to understand why twins run in the first place.

But through the experience of running, through the experience of soul shock, the runner will eventually evolve a new perspective and return to the twin flame relationship prepared for all the new challenges it has to offer.

The runner/chaser period is perhaps the most challenging period in the twin flame relationship; during this time, one of the twins will run from their emotions and the connection while the other will pursue it regardless.

Probably the best description of the twin flame phenomenon is an intense, deep connection that is all that you have ever wanted to experience in romantic love, which then just doesn't seem to get off the ground until you have finished the work this attachment is triggering you to do.

Twins mirror each other and help each other confront their fears as well as deep, repressed desires. Once they are united together, they are stronger than they could have ever been by themselves. There will be obstacles before this relationship can come to fruition; seemingly there will never be the right time, but the right thing at the wrong time is the wrong thing.

And the path to the reunion to become one again is possibly the most intense odyssey you can experience with another person.

CHAPTER 7

Obliviate

MANY PEOPLE MISTAKE THE TWIN flame relationship for an ideal romantic connection where two people who are made for each other meet get married and live happily ever after. The end.

But there is another story, one that comes long before 'happily ever after'.

We didn't think we would miss what we didn't remember; we thought we were here alone. But the soul memory of our twin soul is so powerful that it can make us feel very alone in this world, as we seek for 'that' which is missing.

The paradox is that when you aren't with your twin you are always looking for the 'one'; when you find your twin you think they are love, they are the 'one' and then you are inclined to chase the dream and assume that you deserve that love, and everything will magically fall into place. But it's not always that simple.

We knew we would forget this love once we came to earth, that we'd take on fear and shame and worries and all the human patterns, but we were so confident that we volunteered to come here anyhow.

Most twins entirely forget why they are here until awakening starts rattling them back again to their true soul selves. We had to forget everything in order for us to understand the human condition, to assimilate, to understand how almost every person on earth feels incomplete, separate and is seeking wholeness and love without ever finding it.

You might think twin flames have just met here for the first time in the real world, but this isn't really their first meeting. First of all, they are called 'eternal lovers', and that is for a good reason. They've spent many lifetimes together in the spiritual realms before reincarnating into this physical world. Therefore, when they kindle for the first time, they feel an instant belonging to one another.

It can happen that you may not find them in this lifetime or it's possible you may already have or might have had to let them go because fear stood in your way.

Just like someone blinded by a faraway light, many twins are so absorbed and preoccupied with the problem of the twin flame connection that they're oblivious to the love that's really there in front of them.

And it's not because they are not smart, or lovable; it's because of overthinking, over analysing.

There is fear of the intensity of the twin flame relationship, fear of having their perception of the world transformed overnight, fear of heartbreak and pain. But fears fade away sooner or later, and all runners stop running eventually.

The chaser senses something big just entered their lives, so if they are aware of the connection, why run indeed – but the answer to that is probably more ridiculously simple than what you thought. Fear.

You will try to seek for an answer to why they would walk away from such a sacred connection; you will rewind again and again in your mind each moment, each memory to look for clues, but you can't find any indications for this foreseeable event.

Please don't take this wrong; your twin has strong, intense feelings for you that are undeniable, but they are also freaked out and terrified by everything that's happening. Most times one of you will run away from the other because you haven't gained enough wisdom in life; you didn't do enough stupid things, and this particular situation is just happening too early in life.

Finding the bottom ground of separation will make you feel better. It will help you understand what went wrong; it will bring light to you whether there is something you should feel guilty about; it will help you recover sooner and become a wiser person.

Once twin souls have met or are connected in this life, there is often physical distance between them or long periods of separation that occur. Twin souls may live far away or even reside in different continents of the world. Unique conditions can often prevent twin flames from being together oftentimes. It might also be something that prevents a romantic relationship between them from forming, or something that makes a romantic relationship difficult to maintain.

Of course, other dynamics can be involved; they may be from different races, different parts of the world or age ranges. There are exceptions, but often there are big age differences.

Other reasons why runners run include being committed to an existing relationship, social pressure from friends and family or, and this is a big one, fear.

What seems to happen when all these things come to the surface for clearing and processing is that the masculine side is usually the one who runs first. If they are already in a relationship, if already connected with someone in some way, they generally run straight back into that.

In a twin flame relationship, regardless of gender, each twin contains masculine and feminine energies, but one twin has more yin energy while the other more yang energy. It is not gender discrimination, but the difference is present on a soul level.

A twin flame runner could be a twin with either masculine traits or feminine traits. The one that carries more feminine energy struggles more than the one carrying more masculine energy because generally the masculine side is obsessed more with controlling things, while the feminine side compensates with the emotional aspect. They are the ones that feel something extraordinary has happened, and they are willing to trust this unknown feeling and generally go with it.

They might find it more challenging to deal with the emotional elements of the connection maybe because the feminine energy is more of an emotional creature and tends to be more intuitive, more willing to embrace the unusual, is not so analytical and not so geared into the mind as the other side.

Anyone who is in this situation must know that there is no way to fast-track through this.

The yang, masculine energy, just doesn't know what hit it; it is more concerned with earthly problems and responsibilities and more likely to cling to those circumstances and more inclined to run.

Yin energy carriers in the meantime end up in a bubbling mess by this point, because they have followed their hearts, followed their emotions, and they haven't seen the end result they hoped for. So, to compensate, some tend to hold on to the connection. Others will be driven inwards and really start to look at themselves and get back in touch with who they truly are but without connecting to their twin.

Because it's not just them, it is us too; many females need to adjust to the expectations and conceptions they hold about what a male is supposed to be, think, feel and act like. For twin flames it is essential to get past any three-dimensional stereotypes and preconceptions, because these become powerful blocks to their union.

They probably have too many expectations from the other twin; because they feel this immense love for this person, they are willing to go with the flow of this emotion and in some cases risk or walk away from everything.

Sometimes twin souls do become romantic partners or spouses, but this is often not the case. So please don't count on it. In fact, relying on it means you are missing the point of the journey.

If separation was a result of deliberate action, you can always explore the underlying reasons that caused the separation, and deal with them. At times, the separation may be through activities beyond your power, so the best you can do in such circumstances is to accept your new situation and make the most of it.

It's hard to describe the amount of suffering that is felt when that happens, and sadly, most twins seem to have to go through this experience.

The first step in overcoming the grief associated with twin flame separation is understanding why the separation happened in the first place. You might have different spiritual needs right now, and your twin flame is just not equipped to deliver on those needs.

This can be heart-wrenchingly difficult for the twin flames, which hold within them an unconditional love for one another.

They often harbour a feeling of not being good enough for their partner, that their presence is tainted and hurtful. That the other twin is pure and that they are damaging you or doing you injustice merely by touching and interacting with you.

Fear drives twin flame runners; they run because they are scared of the twin flame journey, of changing their perspective and of all the things that the twin flame journey entails, but they have all the same challenges, all the same pain and all the same fears.

Fear has many sources; there are many types of fears at play that can invade their mind: fear of getting rejected, fear of not being good enough for them, fear of abandonment, fear of losing yourself or the other person, fear of love, fear of things not working out and many more.

All normal relationships have fear attached to them: fear of losing the other person, fear of doing something wrong that might upset them, fear of getting hurt, fear that the relationship might end.

But in fact, love and fear are on opposite sides of the energy spectrum; there is no fear in pure love. The two cannot exist at the same time and space.

If your twin is pushing you away, know that it's not really you that he or she is trying to get away from; it's an unconscious projection of others he or she had a conflict with or felt hurt by. What is going on between you is a mirage overseen by your soul in order to heal and release the original trauma. And if things aren't looking the way you want them to right now, you need to resolve that from the *now* moment because this is all we will ever have.

When separation occurs, it feels as if a part of our soul has been ripped apart from us and we are left falling into never-ending darkness.

Separation, this feeling in itself, is the biggest hurt of all, but our twin is us in many ways. So if we grew up with their families, patterns and experiences, then separation is really an illusion. We say separation, but this parting is key to bringing you in close proximity to your higher self, and your higher self is in tandem with your twin's higher self. You are connected at a soul level, and nothing can break that.

Separation is the perfect platform to build yourself into your truest and most authentic self.

By being your own unique self, keeping your own individual identity in all forms, you are not getting lost in the other person. The other person is not accountable for making you happy, you are. And when you pursue and manage your own happiness, then your life is empowered, by taking care of your own welfare and by your partner coming on this journey with you, as you go along with them. If at any time you are a part of the decision of another person's life, ask yourself if this is what you really want and need because sometimes it turns out they might be two different things. With a simple yes or no, by following that which you believe in, you surround yourself with empowerment, and that keeps you away from dark karma.

All this separation sickness could have been avoided if we didn't have to part ways, but this is often beyond our control or cannot be taken into account as an acceptable solution to this situation.

It helps to show appreciation and realise all those changes were necessary to make you stronger and help you understand the fact that your twin flame is not the only source of happiness in your life.

During this period of separation, you may see the number 22:22 as a reminder that no matter what is happening in the physical, in the spiritual you and your twin are one, and your souls love each other unconditionally.

We must face and resolve these fears, otherwise we will always be pushing love away, being fearful of letting it in. When we clear the energy, we remove the basis of fear, so even if you try to go back there in your mind it does not connect; the heavy energy is gone.

It is important to note that this cannot happen via *ego*; in order to open up to true divinity, one must be willing to be vulnerable and be utterly open with their selves. Not out of force but by realising the fears they held on to for so long due to identifying with the body, with the physical life and with limitations. This is when they will be truly open to love.

By taking a closer look at Isis and Osiris, the representation of the Egyptian twin flame energies, we can learn a profound lesson about twin flames. The myth explains how Isis was devoted, patient and trusting as she travelled the world in search of her lost love.

Unconditional love is what led Isis to sacrifice everything in her life and travel far and wide to retrieve the missing pieces of Osiris, as she believed in their universal, eternal love bond. He was everything she believed him to be, and it was worth the journey and hardships to keep this love alive.

This is an important lesson of trust, because the greatest obstruction that keeps twins apart is the constant debating and doubting whether this is a genuine soul love connection. Sometimes we need to have faith only in ourselves, faith that one day someone will come who would be sure that we are the 'one'.

In essence, we all are being called upon to merge into *sacred union* with our beloved twin flames. But when we approach the twin flame connection from a place of fear, need, want, we unfortunately only attract dysfunction. Remember that you came here with your twin to unite in love, and you were sure you could make it.

If things seem hopeless, it might just simply be a matter of finding the right solution and taking the right steps; self-acceptance is a game changer that can really transform this situation for the better.

Because there is this beautiful thing involved between twin flame connections called 'divine timing', it's always supposed to happen when it is supposed to happen.

When you love with all your being, there is no room for fear, no limits, no such things as boundaries. Love takes you closer to your destination, fear pushes you even further away from it.

CHAPTER 8

Phoenix

WE CAN'T ARGUE THAT WE learn pretty well through pain, but is there any other way? I think many of us are better off with a balance between friction and compassion in our love life.

We run away from chaos and then wonder why mediocrity bores us. The energy between twins isn't called 'flame' for nothing; it cannot be contained and it can't be tamed like a wild beast; it can burn like wildfire and turn everything to ashes. But it can also force you into becoming a whole new person, emerging out of the dust, like a phoenix, and this is ultimately what needs to happen in order to unite with your twin and become one.

When your soul is immersed in the fire, it does not burn; only those parts that are not truly you wither to ashes.

On some level, I think we all know that challenges and failures are what help us grow more than anything else, so can karma help us develop by challenging us in the ways we need challenging.

We are excessively drawn to them because to grow we need to be challenged, even though this usually doesn't seem to be a conscious process and choice. We are pulled towards these heavy partnerships because that is the only way we can confront our monsters and pass the tests we failed to master, in order to leave this relationship behind and evolve and have a more fulfilling life.

One of the biggest lessons karmic relationships teach us is self-worth; shy girls and insecure guys are more at risk of getting wrapped up in an unhealthy relationship. At some point in our lives, we encounter a karmic partner who pushed us to the ground so that we could rise again.

In a genuine sense, twin flames are spiritual moths, souls crawling around in our mortal selves, lifetime after lifetime, like caterpillars who are just being caterpillars. Then, when awakening happens, we enter the cocoon of our metamorphosis.

They are the messengers of the art of transformation, metamorphosis and a higher evolution of self. When moths appear on your path, you are being reminded of your infinite self, that you are being the light; you are being shown that you are in the process of transformation and that you should trust your higher wisdom.

Then, through the spiritual journey, we become butterflies of our spiritual evolution, with one soul body and two beautiful wings. We fly with the grace and beauty of angels upon the winds of unconditional love, inspiring and changing the world.

When the spirit animal of a butterfly enters your life, it augers a time of important change, physically and emotionally, which will transform your life to a higher recognition of yourself. Times of transition draw butterflies to us, reminding us to be positive and rejoice in the change, opening new doors and presenting new opportunities.

Butterflies often gravitate around lovers; they are magnetised by the true love energy created between the two people. Butterflies can also be used by a past loved one to send you a message of love and joy, letting you know they are safe.

Sometimes one or both of you will undergo the 'dark night of the soul', either prior to the meeting, during your connection or immediately after. The dark night of the soul is an intense period of deep inner spiritual growth and soul contemplation that can be accompanied by emotional pain, mental confusion and even physical loneliness. The dark night acts as a type of spiritual initiation, or rebirth, and can, most of the time, bring about a profound shift in consciousness, soul growth and transformation.

To become complete and accept ourselves as we are, we need to embrace all our emotions, particularly those we are the most afraid to admit. Since you are not attuned with your conscious selves, you will speak a different language than you do with other people, you communicate instinctively.

Even when you are in an unawakened state, not spiritually awakened to the bond between you and your twin flame, you still tend to feel a deep sense of knowing them, as if you have known them for ages — an indescribable bond which you can't really put in words.

The real motive twins cross each other's paths is to help each other face their authentic selves.

The dark night — we all wish it was only a night, but as it happens, more or less, it can be suffering that often extends over a period of time, that can make you feel hopeless, helpless and question your life decisions.

You feel confused, angry; you're in agonising pain with dark energy surrounding you, and it can feel that there is no way out of this — a very distressing experience indeed — but it can lead you to huge soul growth without you even realising it.

When twins are together, there is always an intense connection; the soul feels the spark, and every atom of their body vibrates. A new form of spiritual awareness that disturbs is felt at a soul level.

Ascension is in many ways a path to discover where you've put limits on yourself; it's a chance to start over and rise up into a higher state of self. It's actually a beautiful thing, a sign that your soul is desperately trying to open up to you, to something more, to awaken you to your real potential. Try to embrace this perspective, and you can start loving this journey of rediscovering. You are divinely shedding your skin off, layer after layer of limitations, and unveiling radiant love, attracting unity with your mirror soul.

It affects both twins, but differently. The awakened twin will initially chase the other twin and, when that fails, will at some point sink into the depths of this depression, also referred to as the dark night, which is itself part of the ascension process.

Awakening means that the baggage we took on from an early life, the negative lower frequencies from our bloodlines, begins to be purged.

What usually sets off this process is the activation of the heart chakra and kundalini energy rising; it gets triggered when twins connect fully for the first time. And it is only through the awakening process that we recognise and remember our twin flame, the one with whom it is our destiny to unite.

The kundalini awakening is one of the effects of meeting your twin flame. Kundalini somehow awakens these energies inside your body, as everything exists within us.

The kundalini awakening process can often cause turmoil and misery and even actual pain as it rises to the surface and makes you ask yourself if there is something medically wrong. As it curls up and reaches our heart, you can feel intense and uneven heartbeats accompanied by deep feelings of empathy, and being easily moved to tears. When it reaches your throat chakra, you can feel pressure, aches and pains in your throat, jaw and neck and find yourself speaking out the truth, or even yelling and demanding things that have been suppressed; whereas when it reaches your third eye chakra it can bring headaches, tingling and pulsation around the brain and skull.

During awakening you might even be fortunate and be able to connect energetically to your twin, to alert them into knowing who you are and that you are here to unite with them.

The reason the two of you haven't connected physically yet is that there is still work to do, emotional, psychological and spiritual work, including releasing any old soul agreements.

Sometimes the ignition happens through intimate physical union; however, it can also occur during dreams, online contact or hearing their voice. It can happen any way your energies are connected.

Kundalini awakening is a gradual process, and the symptoms leading up to the energy reaching the crown chakra produce self-realisation and enlightenment that can take years. And even more years if twin flames have not consummated their 'marriage' or bonded physically, since it is their alchemical union which helps bring on a balanced union on all levels.

The encounter with this person will trigger a deep and profound spiritual transformation sooner or later, and kundalini awakening lays down the path for this transformation.

Don't think that just because you've cast a beautiful spell of positive energy, nothing will penetrate that shield. You may not be meant to lie down on a safety net all your life, so when karma comes, it will smash to pieces everything you've built and throw you on the right path.

Twin flames mirror issues that need to be worked on and toss in your face all the deep buried issues in you, pushing you to work on them.

As the energy works through your chakras, when the final chakra, the crown chakra, opens, you might experience a full blooming of your consciousness, a sudden big bang type of expansion as you become aware of the divine light within you. This is accompanied by temporary paralysis, as well as intervals of ecstasy, love, compassion and feeling blissfully happy, to the point that you may become completely overwhelmed by your consciousness if you allow it to.

For one person, the spiritual journey can be a torture, for another it can be paradise; it depends much on your energetic baggage, karma, mental patterns and core belief systems.

The truth is, if your twin is running, it's essentially you who are running from yourself. If you are separated from your twin, it's because something is still going on inside of you.

The issues that keep coming up, again and again, will keep showing up until you are ready to truly face them, to be honest with yourself; don't try to figure it out with your mind, go deeper.

You can't get fixed by words; the truth is that you are your own saviour. Many are still wearing a mask, hiding from themselves, staying on the surface when the answers, the transformation, lie much deeper.

Because as long as you keep running from yourself and are full of unconscious disorder, old fears, outworn beliefs and counter intentions, chaos will continue to be reflected back to you with your beloved other self.

And the more you direct your attention to outside situations, trying to fix them, you just end up pushing more energy into it and reinforcing the problem by focusing your thoughts and your words on it.

All this while the real wound festers within. It is no coincidence that the phoenix is a sign of the twin flame, a pair of mythical birds who die only to be reborn into the new fire from their own ashes.

This is an otherworldly journey, and the path goes within the dark forest of your monsters into the light at the core of your being.

Your ego will deny that there is any healing that needs to be done, but when the quietness of the night subdues your mind, your soul will start to whisper.

So today, resolve to do something differently by stopping running from your own darkness, by getting to know what really lies inside you.

You will be questioning everything you've ever known, and you will discard from your life what you no longer need. It can even happen on a subconscious level or things will get in your way, and you won't be able to afford to do any longer some things you used to love in the past, like going out or travelling.

Your attitude towards life might change; you might prefer complete solitude for a while in order to put your thoughts together.

Your attention might be turning in the right direction away from the false beliefs that no longer resonate with you. It might seem as if everything is falling apart, that nothing happens the way you want, but things are being cleared for a higher purpose. You are making room for something new to enter.

Then as your twin integrates the shadow, as they heal those wounds and traumas that come up for them to look at, they become more attracted to the initial runner, as they now hold more light inside of them and are making progress on their mission.

Although some speculations state that twin flames aren't always necessarily meant to have a romantic bond, this might be the case only if it isn't time yet to complete their union. But if it's time and they have completed the journey, you won't have to struggle to make them decent people because they already are.

The dark night can happen at any time after you have met, but oftentimes it begins when you realise there is a real connection between you two because unless you feel a side of you is missing, you will never reach out to find it.

Your life might change profoundly. After meeting your twin flame, romantic relationships can be especially dramatic. You are never quite the same after bumping into your twin because it may be unlike any other relationship you've previously had in your lifetime. A twin soul connection can transform one from the inside out, or even lead to a total meltdown of your life as you have known it prior to that point.

Above all, know that the twin flame journey is not meant to be painful or hurtful; the universe is not forcing you to learn through suffering. But it will grow dark before the dawn.

Sometimes when there is a significant shift in energy, you would get this realisation moment, this light bulb moment when your etheric body energy will shift up a level, almost like an upgraded shield.

Each person's life path is as unique as his or her fingerprint, as is the karmic lesson that he or she needs to confront. You get to experience human reality in all its shades, and from it, you will find forgiveness, compassion and personal empowerment.

Although the hardest thing now will be accepting your new self, it's only from the ashes of the fire of love that a new you can rise.

CHAPTER 9

Backgammon

ONE SOUL, TWO PLAYERS, EACH with two sides – one is light, one is dark.

Your partner will be different from you in all the right areas to bring out new and exciting qualities in each other. Frequently, a twin flame will be the exact opposite of what you are looking for in a partner, but they are time and again exactly what you need in order to transform and feel that you are complete within yourself.

Unlike the more traditional idea of a soulmate, twin flame relationships are based on give and take, are hot and cold and black and white rather than made up of similarities between two people which is more often the case in common relationships.

Twin souls are a perfect representation of yin and yang, two perfect pieces of a puzzle, the same yet different. It is when these two opposite energies collide to form a whole that they transform each other. You are like two magnets, constantly attracting each other. So it makes perfect sense for you two to propel each other when there is inaction within your lives; you are two puzzle pieces trying to fit into each other.

The bond between twin flames is about being able to connect and disconnect at the same time. They can draw out the best and worst in one another. When there is harmony between twins, when there is positive energy, it can be wonderful; it can feel like heaven on earth. But when there is disharmony, it can be intensely painful and can have devastating effects. When there is conditional love or any negative energy forces between twin flames, it can feel like hell on earth.

In the beginning, you are like two north poles being pushed towards each other; you will repel but also attract one another. That is why when twin flames meet, those hidden parts of themselves become visible, as the other side of the soul embodies everything that was repressed.

The moment you meet, the game of hit and run begins; the collision is made, you crash into each other and get pulled right apart again.

But if one magnet stops being a north pole, then it does not matter whether the other is still north pole or not; the meeting is possible.

When that happens, the one who has healed can take upon themselves, with ease, all the problems of the other twin and help them heal. They do so by providing the other twin with the required freedom to be who they really are – their true self.

Whatever it is we are trying to conceal deep inside, whatever we keep buried in our souls and never want surfacing, will rise to the surface. Twin flames will bring forth all our deepest fears, as they embody everything we keep denying within ourselves.

This way we will meet face to face with our blockages, whether it is our fear of abandonment or suppressed passionate desires. If you are afraid of your own sexuality, they will embody everything you are subconsciously uncontrollably attracted to; if you are afraid to take risks, they will be risk takers. There are two separate sets of traits twins possess, two separate sets of characteristics that complement one another.

You will feel drawn to them like there's nothing you want more than to be in their presence, and you won't even know why because they are not your type. Even if you don't even have a type, they are still not your type. There is no logical explanation as to why you are drawn to them of all people.

More than attraction, it is repulsion at the same time as your bodies are adjusting that energy at your own speed, in your own way and in your own time. At times you will be so out of alignment that your twin energy will literally be something you need to get away from; at other times you will be so aligned that you simply cannot be apart.

If you're in a romantic relationship with a twin flame, then it can seem painful at times. Sometimes when the relationship ends, or when both twins mutually wish to part ways, a powerful and magnetic force seems to draw them right back together again. Your paths cross again because it's meant to be, because your soul is 'One'.

You two are one of a kind, not alike, but you are a pair, opposite sides of the same coin.

When twin flames finally cross paths, you will be drawn to each other in ways that are too complicated to explain and can't be reasoned with, no matter how hard you try to rationalise things. It's almost like you're interacting with your subconscious in the flesh. You will feel like a metal object pulled towards a magnet, whether you want this consciously or not. You feel each other's presence and sense you can communicate without words. They somehow perfectly comprehend the experiences you've had when everyone else would only sympathise or flat out say they didn't understand.

If the energy between you is not appropriately balanced sometimes, that can be a problem, because if both of you are very short tempered and you're both very stubborn, then you can't function properly. You need someone to give you the time and space necessary to calm down and talk calmly with you.

But you and your twin flame don't have arguments because you understand each other; you know that they will always be there, no matter what happens. Sometimes, words aren't necessary because you can understand one another without even having to speak. Just one glimpse is enough, and your twin flame knows what's happening inside you. They don't ask too much. They just know.

The main difference between ordinary love and twin flame love is that in the first one, you need to touch base with your problems; you need to sit down with your partner each and every time you have an argument and talk things through because there's no way the relationship can actually function without good communication.

Surely, they can get married to someone else and seem to have their life in order, but they will always remember you. They might even compare them to you, look for your qualities in that person, even go far as looking for people who physically look like you, simply because a piece of their twin soul is in them.

Men and women are united by the forces of female and male energies. If you have more masculine vigour in you and suppress your feminine side, you just can't attract a man with strong masculine qualities. Your energy sources are similar, but they don't fill up one another. Similar energies can form amazing friendships, sexual connections. But not a fulfilling relationship because he just cannot respect or appreciate you, because you don't have what he needs. He seeks balance, which will make him stronger as a man. Your masculine aspect makes him want to communicate with you or have a physical connection, but not appreciate you as a woman.

One may possess all the logic and the other all the emotion: if you're typically arrogant, your twin will most probably be uncertain and quiet. If you're creatively repressed, they will be a flourishing artist; if you're a highly strung individual, your twin flame will probably be relaxed and messy; if you're an emotionally repressed person, your twin will probably be emotionally explosive.

We need to come head to head with the unknown parts of ourselves. As twin flames are two souls conceived from one entity, what one twin soul has in this lifetime is what is necessary for the other to develop. They will have attributes we already have, but while they embrace these traits as part of their personality, we are yet to become conscious of them. Two twin flame souls will be identical, and yet so different. If one is genuinely in tune with their feelings, the other won't be; if one is brave, the other will be residing in the comfort zone. When we accept these differences in them and ourselves, we can heal.

Previous relationship connections might have helped you prepare for the 'one' as sometimes, one's twin may even have or embody some similar characteristics or traits of previous partners, either positive or negative.

What any powerful man with strong masculine qualities is looking for is a woman with a strong female side, a person who knows her worth and respects and nourishes both her masculine and feminine energies.

At the point of precise harmony, where the energies are aligned, the connection flows and hearts are open. When twin flames are out of alignment, the connection distorts and brakes up literally and metaphorically. We are facing the themes on the twin flame journey, seeking harmony and balance between the head and heart, between action and inaction, masculine and feminine, the higher and lower realms.

So when they become aware of the shadow aspects, because now they know what they want, they start to be willing to do the inner work that is required.

This is why it is absolutely necessary that twins go through the separation phase as well.

Meeting your twin flame will probably bring joy and sorrow in equal proportions. Finding your twin flame can be both a blessing and a curse. It's a blessing if you meet and stay together and a curse if the timing is wrong and obstacles get your way, and you are forced to be apart. Anyone who has experienced this life-changing event will attest to its powerful consequences, and it's unlikely that in the end they would regret having this opportunity.

Ideally, they will powerfully transform, as they will finally be able to see and accept who they are as individuals and achieve this transformation. They may have to acknowledge that to compensate for the loss of part of themselves, being separated for so long, wandering without the other half of themselves, they have repressed everything the other twin represents, and these qualities became their shadow side.

The paradox is the more you chase your twin, the greater the distance you will create. The universe has separated you for a divine reason; the thread that ties twins together may stretch and tangle, but it can never be broken. When the divine wills for something to be, nothing in this universe can prevent it from happening.

You are always drawn to each other; no matter how far you run, they are always there. They will find you; it's physics: you are attracted to your opposite.

Your ego will name and blame and suggest that your beloved has never loved you; denial and intuition will be clearly differentiated by the logic of the mind and faith.

You will probably ask yourself time and again why you should have to feel so much love, why you should feel so alive and connected to someone when you cannot actually physically be with them; it seems like a bad joke sometimes.

What brings you together seems to be what pulls you apart, but you will be together again as there is also a force acting that is bringing you closer.

If you have struggled all your life thinking you're typically too much one way and not enough of the other way, when you will unite and merge with your twin, these two sets of traits merge to create one perfect soul.

While residing with your twin flame is ideal, it is not always the case; such connections cannot be ceased or avoided by any rational means. It is an inevitable part of our soul-searching path.

After we accept all those parts of ourselves, that our twin soul is here to help us, then we will be ready for the harmonious love we were eternally looking for with them or with other connections.

However, there is only one person for you in this entire journey of human experience, and only this one soul is going to be your vice, and you its versa.

CHAPTER 10

Would You Look into the Mirror?

Whatever our souls are made of, his and mine are the same.

—EMILY BRONTE (2015), *WUTHERING HEIGHTS*

AND IF YOU DO, WHAT does the mirror show you — is that really you? As life passes by, we are not the same person we once were; we change, and sometimes we become the things we don't want to be. That's why it is good to keep our character in check.

When your reflection is someone you don't know, then who is that staring back at you?

Your twin soul is someone who is like a mirror to you; everything that you feel, they feel; everything that you go through, they experience in the same way. Our twin is here to show us how to grow, how to get over our fears and how to transform our life for the better. It's the relationship we've all been looking for even without knowing because it's all about honouring each other, giving and receiving respect, and exchanging mutual, undeniable love.

When you look in a mirror and wave to yourself, your right hand becomes your left. Twin souls are the same; they mirror one another in polar opposite ways that complement each other.

And when we encounter our twin flame, they reflect those parts of our being that we are not proud of and we are forced to see ourselves naked, without pretence, not what we accept about ourselves, but what we don't. By reacting to their flaws and bad side, we respond to our own, as it is these very traits we keep judging and rejecting.

In each twin soul there is something that inexplicably pulls the other, and this goes both ways. Our twin has characteristics that we don't possess ourselves and the other way around; they are here to show us something that we reject about ourselves, something we still need to accept, develop within, to feel whole.

Usually, it is our shadow aspect we experience when meeting our twin soul. They embody it, and that is why we see ourselves in them. And they see hidden parts of themselves in you; they are forced to fully understand themselves in another person, in another part of them, and it is those other qualities that will trigger transmutation.

One thing is for certain – when we find our twin flame, we are pulled too deeply into love, and dive into all that we were afraid to embrace about ourselves. This fear comes from self-judgment, and it is these parts of us that we reject, that we see as bad or wicked, that make self-acceptance so hard.

When you encounter your twin flame, at last, nothing will be the same again.

Twin souls can each bring out the light and darkness within each other; they can bring out old unresolved problems or unhealed wounds out from within each other, as well as push each other's buttons like no other can. Being conscious of this twin flame dynamic can feel like one is coming face to face with one's soul, for better or for worse.

It is absurd because your twin flame is your mirror, but with someone else's mind. What drives the separation between you is your mind because you cannot help but recognise your soul in another body.

This is the root cause of twin flame separation; they do not run from their counterpart, but from their own mirror reflection. If your twin is running, they are ultimately running from themselves, from their reflection, not from you.

In order to stop running from themselves, they must heal those deep-seated wounds that are holding them in shame and guilt and pain. If you fear rejection, your twin will reject you, which will open the door to the darkness you kept hidden.

Although both twins are each other's mirror image and there is a lot of chemistry between them, the relationship is quite complicated, and they separate.

Through this cruel process, we heal our wounds, as we no longer have to compensate for the loss of the other half of our soul. And the want to heal and do the same for the other person comes naturally, even though their behaviour may be something we would criticise so passionately in others.

Separation is triggered pretty quickly even before you have hardly known each other in the physical realm. The chaser-runner dynamics get triggered easily, and often you don't get to date as in conventional earthly relationships.

Not all twins split, but for many it becomes tough for one or both to coexist together. It's the ebb and flow that gives us time to recover and learn from the relationships that end up in hurt and confusion.

The karmic fields they have been tapping into since birth is one of the reasons many have shut their hearts, and instead they use sexual connections as a means of intimacy because they are so afraid of giving into their hearts.

Separation happens as the mud hits the fan and their emotions are affected. As those start to be triggered, they have to clear it, and that is no easy task when you have to confront your biggest, darkest fears and what they embody.

Sometimes we're confronted with emotions not only from this physical life but also from times past; it's complex, to say the least, and it is almost a wonder that twin flames manage to get through this and find each other.

These types of relationships confront us with our very fears and ego-driven desires, but they aren't just about what's inside; they are also about how we interact at each level and aspect of our life.

With twin flames it's more like how you are dealing with a baby — they are going to ignore you, probably hit you, not hug you when you want, cry, say they don't love you, hate you, run away, but you still know they need you, that you are connected and they love you.

If we can't learn to see our twins for who they are as individuals and as souls on a deeper level, how can we truly open up to them?

But the more you get to know them, the more your illusions drop away. The silliness and irrelevance of all the things we hold dear to our hearts become apparent, and they get discarded in the way a growing child lets go of his toys.

Your twin flame is far from being the perfect partner so often depicted by this term. Your twin flame is instead your perfect mirror.

People and especially your twin flame are not who they pose to be on social media; they are not their actions and nor are they always their words.

What is brimming beneath the surface and going on in their minds when they act, or express things, is not always the truth, nor does it mean they are the wrong person or a bad person.

You honestly and truly cannot know for sure who your twin flame is as a person unless you spend time with them and get to know them and what makes them tick, just like with anyone else in your life. And if you're judging who they are simply by what you see, you are heading down a path that keeps you two in separation by being this way.

Many of you who are on the twin flame journey are in close proximity to your twin, and many of you are not, so all you have is what you see, read or even hear from others about your twin; this can and does form judgement, create suspicion and will break your heart.

Many of the things we presume are the truth about our twin, in fact, are not even close to who they truly are. What we see online and hear from others much of the time is conditioning from their life experiences. Quite often, they do and say things with a cryptic meaning, leaving us to figure out just exactly what they're trying to do.

And what they are trying to do is show you that you are their twin flame, for all intents and purposes. So let down your guard and the walls you have built to keep them away and allow love in. They have no intention of hurting you on purpose or driving you nuts; that is not who they are. They are trying to get you to let love in by getting you to love them on the soul level without the 3-D judgement and the so-called rules that you apply to everyone else you encounter in this life.

I would like to be able to say that this is an easy task, but unconditional love for your twin can come only when you learn to let go of what you think, see and presume as supposedly true. In these cases, seeing is not believing.

To renew our life and be happy, there are specific lessons we need to learn, and our twin soul will assist us with that task. These transformations will be life changing and most likely painful, so you will go through a period in your life where your feelings and thoughts might seem chaotic, stirring up all the hurts and making you conscious of your wounds. When we start confronting our shadow side, internal blockages and negative patterns of behaviour will surface, and it will cause a chain reaction from the other twin. This is a genuine path to learning about true love, selflessness, kindness, forgiveness and empathy, and you will discard anything that is limiting you, such as jealousy or possessiveness.

If your twin seems to express all the worst of the masculine shadow traits, know it's not just an accident; he's not a wicked soul or destined to hurt you for life. He may actually be sensitive to energy and is reacting to the powerful purge of negative energies.

Look at it as projecting. Your twin may be experiencing hate and anger at himself in this situation, but you feel each other's energy. Whatever dark situation your twin may face, whichever sin they may have to deal with, avoiding the problem will only cause more distort, pain, and anger. If both twins are going through a cycle of pride, envy and hate, these are good and bad cycles like the night and day, made to face themselves to the very bone. These emotions are laid bare and come with full force; there is no escaping them, and if these negative feelings also exist in your twin, it is okay for them to express them to be released. We bottle and accumulate so many feelings in ourselves, especially those that society sees as bad or negative.

The twin flame journey is about growing and accepting yourself the way you are. To have a twin is a very special kind of love. It is certainly self-love first because we share a soul; to love yourself is to love your other half. Practice self-love; this is so important. Fall in love with yourself, be your best friend and, after overcoming your fears and dropping expectations, you will be closer and closer to self-love.

That's what the journey is all about, and that means sometimes you find out things about yourself that you don't really like, things you don't want to accept; it can be that unknowingly you make your twin face things that they can't take. And then sometimes it is easier to hate the other than to do the actual work. So don't take it personally, because it isn't about you but about them.

Learn about self-compassion; you have to become love itself first before there is any notion of union with your twin flame or any other. You can't rush this, it takes time, and this you do for yourself and not just to get into union.

By doing your inner emotional work, knowing who you are, what you truly want, what makes you truly excited about life, you find yourself firmly on the path intended for you.

If you don't know those things when the unexpected comes, when life turns a corner without your knowledge, life can get dramatic. If you avoid taking ownership of your personal issues and the emotions in your life, a lesson is created, and that is karma.

Balance in your relationship is where you are not pushed around by the emotional imbalance of others. You are aware of your own unique self, the direction in which those steps take you, and when you are in that place your relationship will reflect that. It's not about self-righteousness; it's about ownership of your inner and outer balance, either with them or with someone like them.

Changing your twin flame relationship and the dynamics of it can only come from changing yourself within.

It comes from balancing mind, body and soul to create the best you possible, doing the work needed, because if you don't change, your twin won't change either.

You need to do your own work first and change, and that will provide the energy that you send out to the universe that in turn will allow your twin, in their own way, to focus on changing themselves.

The twin flame dance is the one that follows periodic fission and fusion. The fission happens when the twin flame aspects go out of balance; fusion occurs when they reach equilibrium again.

In twin flame relationships that are in the process of healing and balancing, it can seem like an energetic dance between the twin flames as they move back and forth, away and towards each other, time and time again. They make you feel mentally inseparable; it's the two of you against the world. You will never stop looking for that feeling you had. No other love can compare to your own twin flame.

If you are not prepared to continue or to embark on your own soul journey, a journey to the centre of yourself, then meeting your twin flame can be excruciating and cause great turmoil. There is work for you to do as you meet your own shadow. It won't be all fun and roses; there are lessons to be learnt.

In the karmic and soulmate relationship, you will want them to be the 'one'; in the twin flame relationship, you know they are the 'one' but think it cannot be them.

It seems like you have this profound bond with each other, which must be destined, but you come into each other's life at the wrong time, or something else stands in the way of your being together. It is not that this is destined to be ill-fated, rather it is a sign that you're not meant to be with each other the way you think you should.

This is not only the most grown-up relationship you have ever had in your life but also the most childish; you feel grateful and happy even for the simplest things; you start seeing life in its purest form ever. There's nothing more beautiful than that – it's perfect balance.

But, in fact, love does come with a certain amount of selfishness in the best sense of the word, having the capacity to stay connected to yourself in the presence of the other.

It unlocks a desire to express individuality and leads people to seek changes in their choice, but that choice also depends on the cultural assumption about it. Self-expression differs across cultures and being denied one's freedom to choose has different psychological consequences as well.

Studies have shown that having one's choice usurped even by those close to us can be disheartening for Europeans and Americans, whereas choice made by a close other can be stimulating for the East Asian.

The importance of expressing *oneness* influences not only what people choose but also how people choose. We often seek variety in our choice making, and this is related to our desire to appear unique. We care about our freedom to choose and care about what we choose.

Self-expression in a cultural context leads people to make particular kinds of choices and develop strategies in order to make sure that those choices reveal something about themselves.

We may idealise Adam and Eve's pretransgression life in the Garden of Eden – a life with no pain, no worry, no fear, no sin, no alienation. But where knowledge to distinguish good from evil is lacking, so is wisdom; growing and maturing requires endeavour, risk and the presence of sin.

Without eating the forbidden fruit, how could they discover honesty if there was no benefit from lying? How could they learn to be brave if they had nothing to fear? How could they express empathy in a world without suffering? Their choice embodies all the complications of humanity's ability to seek wisdom, and in their choice, we face life and mortality with all their ramifications.

Fate doesn't decide everything people get to choose.

It's a spiritual illusion many on earth still have that life 'happens' to us, that we have little or no choice in our experiences and that there is a grand destiny that controls everything. And although it has a say on how the maze of your life begins and ends, how we navigate this is entirely up to us.

If our destiny already knows our every move and choice, and every decision has already been taken by us, then this is our dream and it's a dream that has already been dreamt. But this paradox does not remove free will. Our soul will not try to steer us the wrong way, and for everything that has ever been it will always be right.

As twin flames we are never meant to be stuck; we are required to blossom and grow; to make that happen, forget what society thinks of it, forget our fears and our guilt.

And when you learn to be your own unique self, that's when your reflection shows who you are inside.

CHAPTER 11

Soul Contracts

WE COME ACROSS MANY PEOPLE who are easily forgotten; in fact, the vast majority won't play crucial roles in our lives, but some do leave powerful impressions on us and influence many areas of our lives, challenge our emotional and rational selves and ultimately change our lives.

It nearly feels like you were meant to meet in this lifetime with these people who have crucial roles in our journey of self-accomplishment and transformation; they are what some spiritual teachings call 'soul contracts'.

There are the people who come into our lives for a specific reason, a reason we usually are still to discover and may not understand until way after the relationship is over.

Soul contracts are people we connect with, who are here for a reason, that is to teach us how limited our mind can be, to help us learn, heal, grow and acknowledge every part of ourselves and thus to show us the real path to self-fulfilment.

It is believed that twin flames have been destined for each other since the beginning of time. They go their separate ways, grow and are raised up in different environments, but fate brings them back together.

Some signs and synchronicities can be universal across the board; you might also find these signs in other connections because they are strong. Soul contracts that are meant to be in your life still serve a vital purpose just like twin flames do. So the universe will send you guidance, a unique message just for you, to let you know that you are on the right path.

A soul contract is a connection we have with a person, which transcends time, in many lifetimes. Maybe you have met a person and immediately felt a strong emotion connecting to them without knowing why. This person can be a karmic connection, soulmate or twin flame; that's why it can be challenging to distinguish between the two.

This sacred contract is the reason why you have such a strong connection with them, why you recognise each other and why they are part of your spiritual growth. You can be romantically involved with them, but that is not the case most of the times. They can be your friend, a family member or a pet.

A soul that we have a contract with will help us get rid of everything limiting and constrained, everything that is blocking us, and we might not be aware of it. We attract relationships with different people who help us learn about ourselves, sometimes through support and love but many times through challenges. They are here to remove our mask and inhibitions by showing us our real selves. It is these contracts that matter the most, all carrying profound metamorphic energy, and the love they bring is just one of a kind.

We tend to project our needs onto others, from anything we want to achieve in this lifetime, to confidence, love and feeling worthy, accepted and protected. A soul contract is made to help us find everything we need, by teaching us to look within. Soul contracts are made to show us not only the way we understand the world and others but also to comprehend our own needs and desires, our fears and motives. We will learn it is okay to let go of things that are no longer taking us where we would like to be spiritually, mentally and emotionally.

Every individual we have a significant relationship with will teach us valuable lessons that will affect the future of our relationship with others. We will naturally navigate towards change once we realise our behaviours bring out the same patterns that are limiting us. When transformation occurs, we will no longer hold on to old habits we learned. All future connections will be of much better quality. Some relationships will teach us how limiting our anxieties are, some will show us how loveable we are. They will lead us to the future; they are part of a divine plan.

You know it's time to end the soul contract when you feel it's the right thing to do. There is a reason why this specific person became your lover, and there is a reason why you didn't stay together. They had a target in your life, and once that is fulfilled, the contract is ended. The relationship has served its purpose, and the lesson we learned remains.

It is this pattern that will bring to us people we have soul contracts with, and they will come into our lives to help us learn about ourselves, who we are and whom we are destined to become. These souls affect our relationships and life at a deep, profound level, after meeting them, and when karma dissolves, we will never again be who we were.

Most people say that *the* connection between twin flames is never lost, and it is true that it is never lost spiritually and at the heart level, but in other ways it is, as happens with any other relationship.

When you have no choice in losing someone you love, it will leave you forever wondering why, a question that can never be answered, a question that never should have to be asked.

It would probably be more correct to say they are always connected somehow.

Much like the separation phase, there is an energetic dialogue that penetrates all time and distance.

The invisible cords that bind us to those with whom we share deep love can never be severed, even if the souls have gone from the earthly plane.

These souls will bring those significant changes in our lives through a unique connection; they have a particular task, and that is to teach us valuable lessons. Those people we have soul contracts with will come to our lives for this purpose, and they will be an essential and unavoidable part of our unique path.

They can be family members, friends, lovers, co-workers and so on. In other words, we choose to learn from these souls because of the lessons they carry within, and they accompany us on our journey for this specific purpose. This process starts early in our childhood when the ebb and flow of patterns of behaviour will establish our barriers and our primal wounds, just so that we can heal later.

It is these souls who will help us become who we are, affect our relationships in many ways, but more than anything, push us towards awakening, teach us love and how to relate with one another, help us heal and embrace our unique path, and ultimately find our true self. It is not rare for these contracts to carry intense emotions, sometimes very painful. It may seem as if they are here just to hurt us, to put more salt on the wound that needs to heal. But the fact is, they are here to help us become aware of that wound, and find healing within ourselves, instead of suppressing it or denying it, and we have chosen them for this very reason.

Sometimes we repeat these lessons just so that we can incorporate what we've learned, and heal our wounds.

One of the gifts that soul contracts have to offer is love; they show us the path to true love by challenging us and connecting our soul with another. They will show us the way to love. But they also represent challenges and trials we have to go through. This is why some may have many soulmates and karmic partners who carry difficult lessons, and that is solely because everyone has a path that is unique. They will change the quality of our future relationships, as, after each encounter with another soul agreement, we will speak more from the heart rather than from ego and fear.

Soul contracts can be the most intense connections you will encounter that are often full of love, passion and drama because they have many issues to solve from their past lives.

Giving in to the urge to have sex with a karmic connection keeps karma active. Shifting your attention away from sex and seeing that you are in love with them merely because you find them fun and exciting to be with, not because they make you feel whole, lessens karma and its hold on you. If you see yourself having many partners, or feel as though partners are always leaving you, it's a sign that you've surrounded yourself with the wrong people. This is where your life has not found change around the corner; you somehow missed the signs, and you are now wandering around that cornfield.

The attraction is divinely designed so that you won't be able to resist and avoid the lesson. The stronger the physical attraction is, the stronger the karmic experience will be. The chemistry was designed to keep you with that person so that it can help you push through your issues. Because if you really knew of the pain you would go through with that person, then you'll run away screaming. But by having this experience with this person, you've come out to be a better person. Karma will show you where in the relationship you need to be more responsible with your emotions, as in where you need to transform anger, resentment and shame into love, gratitude and joy; it will also show you where your boundaries need to be, and why.

A soul alliance must be based on the understanding that the purpose of a karmic relationship is to support us, shed our old skin and escape limiting behaviours. We can look at these kind of relationships as some sort of spiritual cleansing.

By seeking confirmation in people around you, what you get is a projection from their emotional life experiences. This is divinely designed to not match your truth or your vision. There will always be something in the relationship that will be a red flag, something out of balance.

This relationship can get better only if both of you are willing to grow together and embrace love, grow emotionally and spiritually, be on the same path, work together for the future that you want, both heading towards the completion of your goals and dreams.

When you start developing your life, you might drift away from them because you will be faced with your true feelings about these people and learn how to rise and never look down again.

CHAPTER 12

The One

DURING A WEDDING CEREMONY, SOME vows are exchanged, where each partner agrees to forsake all others, for this 'one' person.

It means this person must have captivated you to such extent that you no longer want to look left or right; you have in front of you everything you ever wished for, so in a way, this 'one' person is expected to meet our every need.

I am the chosen one; I am important; I am irreplaceable; I am your friend; I am your passionate lover; I am your intellectual equal, the one to offer you security, stability, adventure, excitement; I am unique; I am the 'one', and infidelity tells me I am not.

I deserve to be happy. Because of this romantic ideal, we rely on our partner's fidelity, and we have never been more inclined to stay in the relationship, not because we have new desires nowadays but because we live in an era in which we think we are entitled to pursue our ambitions.

This is the first time in history we want love with the 'one' in the long term, not because we want our partner to give us many children because many won't make it through war or illness, not because it is our duty to populate the globe; this is the first time we desire love that is about pleasure and connection.

When marriage used to be an institution, infidelity threatened our economic security, but now that marriage is a romantic relationship, it threatens our emotional security. You think you know your life, who you were as a couple, who you are, but now you question everything.

Karmic relationships are the continuation of past dating habits, which are a product of the intimate relationships you had growing up as a kid and as a young adult. These early relationships shaped your feelings about emotional intimacy.

Life is full of ironies; we used to turn to adultery to find true love, but now that we look for love in marriage, adultery destroys it.

What if there are things not even a good relationship can provide – if even happy people cheat, people who have been faithful for decades one day cross a line they never thought they would pass, at the risk of losing everything, and for a glimmer of what?

When both of you get bitter towards the relationship, have arguments, say hurtful words, do painful things, but neither of you knows why one of you becomes jealous and suspicious that the other is lying, and someone else is filling the emotional void between you, your interactions might still be the same, but the feelings behind them have changed.

One of the most important tests of faith that twins have to face is when they meet under unfortunate circumstances when one or both are in a committed relationship or bound by marriage. A confusing battle between the heart and the mind takes centre stage; karma is created between their values and their behaviour.

When we've experienced something, it's often hard to accept that something else is possible.

Your twin flame is going to smash to pieces all the preconceived ideas of relationships and connections you had so far in your life. Their role is to actually do that, shatter those templates because their vibrational frequency is so high and the loving connection is so strong that it will make you question every relationship you've had in your life.

It may seem a little bit brutal when someone is in a marriage for decades and suddenly a twin flame drops in, and everything is thrown out the window. In some cases, the marriage does dissolve, not because of this twin flame union disruption but because once twins recognise each other, they know and feel that powerful connection. So it may be tough for them to drop from a high vibrational frequency to the conventional energy of their relationship, what some may refer to as falling from a fifth dimension to a third dimension relationship; that's quite a big leap to take, so some of those marriages will come apart.

The running stage – this stage in spiritual evolution seems to be part of the course. When twin flames start running like this, they can run for a very long time – weeks, months, but years is more common – and sometimes they don't get back together at all. By that time one or both twins are so entrenched in their old ways of thinking and living that they forget who they truly are. They identify themselves with that persona, and so they go on living that three-dimensional life.

It's much easier to think that a relationship outside of them will make them feel complete rather than doing their inner work and completing themselves. This is how the cycle begins: people start going around in circles looking for love in all the wrong places.

The moment you discover someone is cheating on you, you confront them; if it continues you throw in the towel and walk away. If you spy on them until you have something to wave in their face, then you are stooping to their level and thus creating a karmic connection. A dark path leading to negative feelings of revenge, feeling resentful towards themselves, creates karma for them, but when you engage in retaliation that karma also becomes yours.

If you remove the blame, the judgement, you find that the act of cheating is caused by misalignment. Cheating will not take place if genuine love is consistently present and the cheater is not feeling inadequate in themselves. The truth is that when a person has cheated even to the smallest degree, it's a sign that the relationship won't be forever, and to stay beyond what's comfortable would be destructive. This love has no attachment to indicate how long it will last, what direction it will take or whom it's for.

It can be hurtful if twins share energy with one another, as this is something that you can feel in your chakra and energy system.

You may meet while your twin is committed to someone else. You can meet your twin in different ways, but you will not be able to continue practising this treachery for very long after that if an eclipse is going to happen in this life.

'All is fair in love and in war', and in part that is the bitter truth. Love does not care for time and place, or the rules, agreements and commitments of your personal life; to seize this love, you must be willing to break free from these arrangements and give yourself to your heart's desires.

This is really the most challenging of all the circumstances that twin flames can encounter, when they are already committed to other people.

The soul does not go by the colour of your skin or the age of the physical body; the soul is not interested in whether you are married to other people. The soul is the soul.

You might declare life a big paradox when the person you believe to be perfect for you, to be the 'one', is already with someone else. Till you and your twin realise you are half of the same whole, until that blindfold comes off, years might pass, and in some cases, some of you would have made their life with someone else.

There is no right or wrong when your soul is learning, because all roads lead back to the same route and the direction your soul wants to move forward in.

When the love you have isn't what you want and need, you become a seeker; it's a tricky plight, but there is still hope, although your options are limited. Each twin set's experience will be unique; whether they choose to have an affair or try their luck and wait for them to get a divorce, both these choices have their associated risks.

Choosing the first option can create difficulties and might ruin your relationship with your twin if you try to force them to divorce their spouse.

If you choose the second option, you might end up waiting for something that might never happen, but that may occur with your first choice as well.

None of these scenarios brings you the positive result you are waiting for. Then you need to understand the reasons why the universe has sent your twin flame your way in such unseemly times.

For some it can be a balancing act, feeling this tremendous love for someone, immense chemistry, heart jumping around like mad around them while managing to stay in a conventional relationship. Some can, but the majority of twin flames cannot. I know many twin flames often fear it will only be an affair, nothing will ever change, that they are somehow reading more into this than they should.

Probably the worst in an ongoing twin flame affair is that you are so close to having what you want, but you may never have it entirely because their partner fills the karmic blank even if the marriage is not a happy one.

Harmony is one of the key elements in this journey; it's a tough state to reach, where chances are you will kind of set yourself up for heartache.

After you bond so intensely with someone, you may get a rude awakening after an evening of deep and utter connection when the committed twin has to leave to go home to their spouse.

When you are intimate with your twin, it will be a lot more challenging to keep an emotional distance, to walk away when you get a taste of ecstasy just for the few hours that they are able to give you. You may not enjoy going through this, but there is a whole lot of healing and growth possible if you hang on in there, and not making love with your twin makes that a whole lot easier.

In many ways, it can be pure self-torture because you are trying to feed off from bits and crumbs. The first days of separation will always be the worst if you are sleeping with your twin and you put yourself through this over and over.

What most people don't know about the twin flame journey is that there is not a whole lot of intimacy between twin flame couples initially. Intimacy does happen of course, but this may not serve your highest interest in the long run.

The reason why they aren't so sexually active is that in the twin flame dynamic, with the lining up of the chakras and the rising of the kundalini energy, sex tends to bring to the surface all the subconscious wounding and traumas that are still blocking the chakras. Much of that negative energy comes from not only this life but also previous lifetimes and is stored in the seven main chakras. It can also be kept in the body, but what concerns mental, emotional and vibrational traumas tends to create blockages in the corresponding chakras. It triggers the subconscious wounding for the kundalini energy to rise up willingly from the base-of-the-spine chakra and flow up through all the in-between chakras, rising up to the crown chakra. These focal energy points need to be open and free from all old pain and the distress that blocked it.

Intimacy can be the quickest way to do this, but it's also unsustainable because when all the past wounding and trauma gets brought up for healing, it energetically pushes away the twin, bringing about the push-pull dynamic that twin flames are so familiar with.

When all these feelings are brought to the surface, your system may not be able to handle them. With such an overload of unresolved traumas, you can hardly keep yourself standing amidst all the pain that was brought to the surface at such an accelerated pace.

Your soul gets isolated while conversion begins from inside out, and you better buckle up because you will hit extreme highs and plunging lows.

In normal relationships, you often need sex to seal the deal, especially if you want to keep someone coming back for more but not with this one. It may not feel that way, except this isn't love; of course, this is manipulation. It's your own subconscious triggering the fear of loss and mishandling your sexual power to bond with someone, and that just cannot be a twin flame frequency.

It may feel really good that they can't get enough of you, and they keep coming back despite them being committed to someone else, but that is actually an indication of your own subconscious pain in which you are mixing up your self-worth with your sexual worth. This is a trap especially for women because we are so indoctrinated with the sexualisation of femininity and the false concept that our value is connected to our ability to please a man in looks and in bed.

This is why twins often feel worse after having shared intimacy or having been open with each other; it's because their systems trigger each other to connect in love.

The truth is, however, that it is enough just to feel this powerful energetic connection for the subconscious wounding to be triggered. This way it allows a far gentler release of this stored suffering than when twins release it through sexual encounters.

Sharing the bed with your twin doesn't allow you to step back and be objective, because you are in the middle of other things; it is also much more frustrating because you are both so close and yet so far from everything that you want.

This is because you almost get what you want, but no matter how much you try you can't get them to commit fully.

Your twin choosing someone else triggers fear of loss and beliefs about not being good enough, fear of abandonment, lack of self-love, co-dependency issues, and instead of embracing the pain, you look for someone to take it away and cast upon them your illusion of perfect love, who you now speculate might actually be the 'One'.

When you keep your pants on, you avoid projecting the twin flame label on everyone you share your bed with. Most twins, in fact, are aware of the connection and can't even imagine being with someone else, so most of them remain celibate until they can be with their twin.

It can take a couple of years with other people to realise that there was only 'one' person and not any other up to this point in your life who could grant what your twin gave you.

And even if many years have passed since you've seen or spoken to them, it won't come as a surprise to decide to commit yourself fully to them, to keep yourself only for your twin, to marry the 'one' or no one.

After meeting your twin flame, all your chakras will be readjusted and balanced; you become much more emphatic, and your intimacy levels reach a whole new level.

Meeting the 'one' has opened your heart chakra, and if you are looking for love intimacy with other partners, either that becomes the ultimate letdown, and no one can trump the depth of that connection, or it can be just a fantastic experience based on chemistry.

It is just as if the universe wants to test you, whether you prefer true love or choose to just settle down for some hot sex.

Ultimately, what really brings light to the truth is how you deal with the unknown, the twists and turns that are inevitable on the twin flame journey. Those not ready for what the twin flame journey entails will quickly dump their would-be twin and move on to the next.

Those double-dealing relationships support your union process, and they do so in many ways – for example, by preparing your twin for you. They trigger all your subconscious fears about loss and not being good enough; they help your twin learn lessons they simply can't learn with you. They are not committed to someone else because that person is better than you. If your twin were here now with you, your deepest wound layers wouldn't be triggered, which makes you think someone else could be more interesting, attractive, smarter, better in bed, a more suitable wife, mother, and so on, than you. Don't even fantasise about their fabulous relationship; don't judge it by the happy family portrait they show on social media.

There is no course for envy the constant bickering between them because no matter how much they try, the third party always feels that they aren't the number one in their lover's heart, that they live with someone who is genuinely in love with someone else. Probably there isn't much action in the bedroom either, and if there is, it is probably out of compulsion. It's something that needs to be done, like brushing your teeth. Almost all of them switched off the sexual attraction even when they were happy, before they even met you. That sex is nothing compared with the love you make.

When you are sharing your bed here, there and everywhere, you will not be able to go to the depth of your own subconscious wounding; you will have too much to keep you distracted from going within.

And, of course, there are the ones who have an extramarital affair, who try to justify this to themselves by slapping on the twin flame label. They feel that this being a spiritual soul connection, it is somehow above other earthly connections and is, in fact, superior to the karmic connections in their lives, and this exempts them from having any morals. Twin flame relationships are definitely in a different ball field, but the whole concept of them being higher and more than or in any other way superior to other relationships is an ego concept.

Just because you have identified yourself as a twin flame doesn't suddenly make it right to have an affair when you or maybe both of you are involved with someone else. Being a twin flame does not hoist you above common morals or exempt you from behaving with integrity. If you are sneaking around your partner's back, you're not acting with integrity, and even though you may be truly authentic twin flames, you become each other's dirty little secret that you are hiding from your spouses.

With this frequency, you cannot align in the twin flame eclipse, ever.

So it is important to first end the relationship you are in before you start a relationship with someone else.

But this is not about pointing fingers and feeling awful about it. It does not mean you are a bad person. The gates of hell are not going to open just because of that, but, solely on a law of attraction level, you cannot honestly have what you really wish for when you allow yourself to settle for less.

Remember, everything does happen for a reason; it is always happening for our highest good. If you do find yourself in the middle of an affair, it is because that experience has served you up to now.

The soul does not care if you are married and have ten children, if you're fifty years old and your twin flame is in their twenties. Again, it is going to be different for everyone. There are twins about the same age as there are sets of twins where ten to fifteen to twenty years is the age difference. This does not matter in twin flame connections, because their soul is the same age. The soul does not care what body you are in, how old you are or what your physical circumstances are.

There is a chance that you go through an affair on your path, but having to deal with your own wounds and lessons, you get stuck being the other person, a mistress for years on end without ever getting closer to the twin choosing you.

If you match your twin's fear-based behaviour, then you might decide they cannot possibly love you and act in this way.

But if they are really your twin flame, then they do love you. They just can't take that part of themselves that you, without knowing it, make them face. So just focus on the love they give.

But if you do make that shift completely, don't be surprised when your twin finally pushes through their divorce or leaves their current spouse.

They might have a change of heart and can choose you over their spouse because he or she can't possibly deny the insane magnetic pull between you two.

If your twin is telling you they cannot be with you because they are married and they have kids, they are just making excuses to postpone taking a decision.

In some ways, it's quite simple: if someone really wants to be with you, nothing will stop them.

One usually clings to the marriage or the marriage comes down naturally once there has been a connection with a twin flame and that loving heart has been felt. This is because not being able to go back home and feel that love in the heart with their partner will become insufficient for the twin involved.

They either walk away from the twin flame connection because they literally can't feel what they feel and navigate both relationships or they fall back to the old system of three-dimensional relations set up with the person they were with. Or this is a catalyst and the marriage will end because, in reality, twin flames aren't here to live in three-dimensional relationships; they are meant to have a higher connection of the soul. They are not actually here to maintain a conventional relationship, because that is not what a twin flame is meant for.

They might come into your life out of the blue to make you reflect on a particular aspect of your life that needs resolution. Maybe they came to make you realise that you're spending your life with the wrong person and selling yourself short. People think it's amoral to get divorced, but that's just primitive thinking.

There is nothing to feel ashamed of; no matter what your personal circumstances are, marriage contracts should not hold dominion over you. They are just a common template that must never limit your access to love.

By honouring your commitments with your partner, you might think that they are holding you back from true love, but they actually prepare us for our twin flame because everything that happens in our lives happens for a reason.

These marriages and relationships aren't built to last, but they aid in our spiritual growth. They impart in us certain qualities that are needed for a healthy twin flame relationship. Our intuition tells us to hold on to such relationships because it knows that we still have to learn something from them.

Being a twin flame, you should never feel guilty or wrong about disrupting a marriage. It's hardly a disruption when unions are destined and happy; they cannot be broken up.

It's entirely okay to follow your joy, no matter what people might think of it. There is also the issue of self-love when you are facing this problematic situation in marriage. The universe is aligning your true desires; it is really your choice to ignore or follow them.

But I am not advocating that everybody can run off with everybody. But if you are entirely sure the person sleeping next to you isn't the 'one', the vows you made of pure devotion no longer hold true; you're just standing on a sinking ship.

Sometimes we get stuck by absolute concepts of loyalty in marriage, and even if our feelings change towards our partner, we still carry on in a marriage that has lost its spark because we're not loyal to our spouse but to the concept of loyalty. Then we are captive, and this holds us back from daring to step forward to end a marriage that is draining us emotionally. It is not unusual to feel hopeless and mentally distraught in such situations. There are plenty of people out there who have given up and feel as if they've lost their twin to another person.

There's not a thing you can do or say, including giving them ultimatums that will make them choose you over them. When divine timing is right, when they are ready, they will leave on their own.

You will meet on the way and at the time you both agreed to; they will show up when they are supposed to, not a minute earlier.

At the end of the day, twins come here for a mission, and if other connections and difficulties exist, they have to fit it around that mission; the mission cannot be fitted around them.

You can't bend a twin flame union around anything; whether you can bend the marriage around the twin flame union is another thing.

No other real-life situation will provoke you like this one, and this can very well be part of a script you and your twin made to find your way back to each other or not.

There is no right or wrong when your soul is learning, because all roads lead back to the same route and the direction your soul wants to move forward in.

Living with another person who is not your half can call upon you to demonstrate a real, high level of source love, unconditional love, understanding and empathy for the parties involved but also be mindful of the bigger picture.

Truly loving someone is to give them the space they need to breathe, to let them live up to their own standards and principles, even if it means you don't get what you want immediately or maybe never in this lifetime. And honestly, you don't need sex to keep this one close, because if they are your twin flame, they can't forget you either; no matter whom they are sharing their bed with, you are as deep in their heart as they are in yours.

When your twin has committed to someone else, you have to give them the chance to live up to the man or woman they want to be.

CHAPTER 13

Destination Lost

Darkness cannot drive out darkness; only light can do that.
Hate cannot drive out hate; only love can do that.

—Martin Luther King Jr. (1969), Strength to Love

Your undeniable devotion to this love, as powerful as it is, is not seen by them or as intensely expressed as yours is, and you know this, but you keep going back, hoping things will change, yet they don't.

A karmic relationship is not a soulmate or a twin flame relationship, no matter how much you may want it to be, and this can be difficult, to say the least. It can be a very powerful relationship that can sometimes overwhelm you and cause you to feel defeated and hurt time and again.

When karmic relationships continue for too long, you might start feeling resentful towards the little things that never used to bother you, might even be confused as to where these feelings came from, almost as if they popped up out of nowhere.

This confusion can lead you further into depression and worry, and so the cycle begins. You may feel trapped, scared, unable to move forward.

There will be no easy way out, and it will be entirely up to you what is acceptable in this kind of relationship, when there is no real growth, but much confusion and indecision.

You never seem to be able to let go of past hurt, and it doesn't take long for resentment to turn into anger, rage, obsession, isolation, depression when neither of you can recognise where the change in the relationship is coming from. Overindulging is common in this situation, in any form, may that be alcohol, sex, drugs, food or any sort of abuse. It is not unusual for these connections to become one of the most destructive, toxic and painful types of experiences.

It goes without saying, but if the relationship progresses to the point of verbal or emotional abuse, the debate ends there; not all of us are thick-skinned enough to emerge emotionally whole out of it.

One of the glitches present in many bloodlines is an abusive relationship pattern. This includes not only physical violence but also emotional, psychological and sexual abuse, financial exploitation, blackmail, deprivation, humiliation, blame, threats of harm or abandonment.

And as twins are empathetic souls, they want to help others but cannot do it without self-mastery; otherwise, they will end up hurting themselves and enabling a cycle of dysfunctional behaviours in the process.

This will only attract a 'near' twin to reinforce these patterns, but we are also offered the opportunity to see beyond them until we decide to do things differently.

When a twin is separated from the other, it might seem they want to hurt the other twin, but that is never their intention. As a matter of fact, by this behaviour, they are protecting themselves from rationally trying to reason with their mind, which is pretty much disturbed by this connection.

Separation is a hard burden to bear, but it is the only thing that will force us to look inwards. Your twin seems to cause you nothing but pain in the physical, but what their spirit really aims at is triggering your wounds so that your emotional baggage will dissipate.

This person will push your buttons to the maximum, challenging you to grow. This is what you agreed to do for each other, to help each other's evolution.

This is especially true if in your relationship there is no equality, it's only abusive, it's only physical, there is no commitment, just a lot of jealousy and resentment; they might even want to cause you trouble and try to crush you as you crushed them. If you cannot understand how you fell for all the stories they told you and how you can trust them again, then probably karma has stepped into your relationship.

This feeling of familiarity is inexplicable; being with them will seem so natural, and in such a short period of time you feel as though you have found your home in another person even if there are obvious red flags that point to the possibility of them being all wrong for you.

And it's important to take into account that there is also an unhealthy aspect to this tempestuous connection that is commonly found in aggressive relationships, where the victim is repeatedly drawn to their abuser. It is crucial to realise that just because someone is your twin soul, doesn't mean they should get a free pass to maltreat you, your body, mind and soul. It is not surprising for abused partners to justify the behaviour of the abuser with the concept of twin souls. In such cases, if the relationship is abusive, even if the person is your twin, it is time to withdraw for good and resist the urge to be dragged into such a relationship again.

You'll also be aware that actions between twin flames typically do not tend to be out of malice, cruelty and spiteful vengeance.

If you find yourself in an abusive relationship, the way out is to openly express independence from them, slowly, gently but firmly; by doing this you step into empowerment.

Fear is not rational; it's emotional, and emotions are anything but logical. It's like trying to find the answer to why people smoke, drink or do drugs and get hooked despite knowing it's not good for them.

Our fear can have us behaving erratically and avoidantly, as it impacts our emotional well-being and our sense of security and safety, and it gets hard to enjoy life when we're submerged by fear. It influences how we feel about ourselves, about life, about others. And being aware of this sacred connection does not change that. Anytime anyone treats you from a place of 'less than', boundaries are created.

You twin isn't a bad person. If they did something hurtful, they could have been acting on patterns, others' influence or even based off old negative baggage.

Behind every hurtful action, there is fear; it's because they are acting out hurt themselves.

Trying to put yourself in their shoes may help or not, as you may not have taken the same decisions. Why did they do what they did? Why did they say what they said? There is usually a different explanation than what we've perceived from our perspective of anger.

For example, if someone uses hurtful words, it is often a deep-seated pattern of feelings that they have to defend themselves from others, meaning they are afraid of getting hurt. Remember, we are all souls in human bodies; our actions are a result of the patterns and beliefs we've taken on in life.

If they've been bad, it's not who they are; they are reacting to the negative programming in their system, inherited or absorbed from society.

If you are a parent or a person who takes care of children, you know that even when they misbehave or do something wrong, you do not love those children any less than when they are being good and happy. You do not judge who they are, based on their behaviour. A person, adult or child, is not the sum of all their deeds or actions, good or bad. That is just how things evolve because of things they experience or don't experience, causing the said actions.

This also needs to be how you look at your twin flame.

The actions, reactions and things they may say or do might be hurtful to you or what you may interpret as negative or bad and will cause you to judge them and wish to denounce them for it. Also, it may seem that even their good behaviour and actions can make you upset, making you feel left out by them for not being included in it.

It is a dropping of conditions both for yourself and your twin. Easier said than done, but needed to move forward. It's an understanding that no matter how you disappoint your twin, or they disappoint you, it does not change the love between the two of you.

What is completely obvious to you makes absolutely no sense to your twin; as a matter of fact, they believe you can do much better than this person you are currently with, because they don't treat you the way you deserve. The funny thing is that your twin is often acutely aware of the fact that you deserve much more or even better than the way they treat you. They can't understand their own behaviour because you are the most important person in the world to them, and when you least anticipate it, your twin will step up to remind you why on earth you continue to torment yourself by staying in a relationship with that person despite their odd behaviour.

It's known that there is a difference between an act of bad behaviour and the good of the soul within the person. It's accepting that maybe not today, maybe not tomorrow or next week, but ultimately you will be together, your souls will truly be melded into one.

What you need to understand is that at the core of their being, your twin does love you, thinks of you, desires and needs to be with you.

But they don't know how to get there without letting go of the conditioning they've become used to, and it is the same with you too.

You and your twin soul have equipped yourselves with everything you need to complete your journey back to love; inside of you, you already have the divine blueprint to your journey, and it's not identical to anyone else's. It's something that you feel into, and often you must relax into allowing this inner wisdom to show up. At any given moment you can choose to either feel into the inner light and radiant power of love and move forward from this point, or let the outer stories shared by others dictate your journey, continuing on in darkness.

This journey is not your normal traditional love relationship based on what we've been taught about love, and you need to let go of these rules for any eclipse to take place.

CHAPTER 14

V for Vendetta

Then Amnon hated her exceedingly; so that the hate wherewith he hated her [was] greater than the love wherewith he had loved her.

—2 Samuel 13:15

How can it be that the most profound love can turn so easily into the most intense hatred when separation occurs? The anger often gets expressed in endless arguments over parting arrangements.

The thought of not being with them might have made you cry or made you so mad that you wanted to punch a wall so hard that it came down, or even scream to the universe so much that you desire this to end, but deep down you never truly stop loving them. And sometimes this alone can make you feel very frustrated, knowing that you love them no matter what they do.

All close relationships are characterized by tension because they involve a sacrifice of individual needs to accommodate the requirements of a couple.

Ironically, those prone to disorder might be the ones who sensed something was going wrong early on in the relationship but mistakenly thought expanding their sacrifice was the answer.

They neglect to see that just as it takes two to tango, so it takes two to tangle.

We can find many situations in which people find themselves hating the person they love; at first this may initially appear to be a contradiction, for how can one love and hate the same person at the same time?

Love and hate are often described as opposites and thus it is impossible to talk about hating the one we love without engaging in a rational contradiction.

Love and hate are somewhat distinct rather than opposite experiences; although similar in several aspects they are divergent in others.

In the light of this complex nature of feelings, it is plausible that when people describe their relationship as a love-hate relationship, they might be referring to a different feature of each experience.

People refer to their connection as a love-hate relationship when circumstances are such that they focus on different things, thus the change in the emotional attitude. When they think about their partner's wisdom, they love them dearly. When they focus on the embarrassment they bring upon them, they hate them.

Such dynamics can make sense when emotional experiences are different from external and personal circumstances, which may often change our emotional attitude towards the same person.

Love becomes a fertile ground for hate when love turns sour; when there is no other means of communication with the other person, when all other paths are blocked, it can be a layer of protection in which both closeness and separation are impossible.

There is also no doubt that love can be extremely dangerous, maybe as much as hate, and people have committed the most horrific violations in the name of love.

To claim that love and hate can exist at the same time and place is difficult to explain, especially when they exist not merely at the same time but also over an extended period, as someone may say they dearly love their partner, but in general, they hate them because of their dishonesty. In a similar way, a person involved in an affair might love the married person deeply, while also hating them for still being committed to their spouse. Likewise, we may learn to hate someone because we love them but are unable to free ourselves of the love we feel for them, or because this love is not reciprocated.

It is interesting to observe that a desire for exclusivity arises only in romantic love but not in hate; on the contrary, in hate we want others to share our negative behaviour.

The difficulty arising from hating the one we love can be possible from a logical point of view as it does not certainly involve a contradiction. Although the presence of these mixed emotions is not necessarily puzzling, when present not merely at the same time for the same person, it seems to be psychologically incompatible.

The line separating love and hate is a blurred one; the two are opposites, but share a common thread of passion.

The foundation of our love gets infiltrated by hate when someone we love and care about hurts us emotionally; the pain can often be greater and can lead to hostility if that someone is close to us, whereas the same behaviour on the part of a stranger may only trigger anger and annoyance. This is because we have higher expectations from those dear to us.

Our negative responses are bound to be more intense when people repeatedly inflict unjustified harm upon us.

People sometimes feel such great hate towards loved ones that they are prepared to take revenge in the cruellest way or behave in incredibly spiteful ways towards the loved one who wounded them.

And no revenge is more burning, more sharply personal, than hatred towards a previous lover who has frustrated us, and been false and therefore punished and has thus been turned into a hater.

None of this, of course, shows that love and hate are simultaneously intertwined, but only that hate can rapidly replace love when the love becomes too heartbreaking and complicated.

Psychologists do not even agree that love is truly an emotion; a torrent of excitement, nervousness and ardent exaltation has been matched to a temporary form of insanity or a sweet madness that allows us to overlook our partner's shortcomings, at least long enough to conceive and, if possible, remain deeply attached to them until death do us part.

Hate is sometimes a reaction to the people we have loved and invested most of our time in, a manifestation when a vital agreement of the connection is broken.

One thing is for certain: little good ever comes from hate; more often than not it's a lose-lose situation. What hate does at the time of separation is evident, but maintaining it beyond that point is unknown.

Intense anger follows this egoistical behaviour as they see the departure of the loved one as the loss of something which rightfully belongs to them, the abandonment rage arises from a sense of how dare you do this to me; hence the subsequent need to fight over their possession. Perhaps the greatest predicament people face in these relationships is that they eventually end up competing with one other.

You don't really hate your twin, but it may happen that they make you so angry that you might tell them you do, but that's more of an 'I hate that I love you so'.

Hate is a strong word. I would never say you hate your twin soul: this sounds more like a question that relates to unconditional love, and true twin flames always have unconditional love for each other at a soul level; down there is nothing else but love.

Hate is the opposite of love and would be defeating the purpose of this experience, if it is hate that exists in your connection.

It is true that the pain that exists in somebody can make them seem angry, frustrated and even hateful if you are not prepared for the emotional chaos involved in the twin journey.

When it comes to living physical life, where one or both twin flames are not awakened, such situations can arise.

Love turning into hate is less likely in awakened twin flames because they are aware of the true nature of this connection, and with their awakening, their ego starts dying. Hatred is an outcome of some form of ego/expectation.

In the initial stage of this journey, when ego is a solid part of twin flames' energies, when there are still negative blocks present which need to be cleared, then emotions like anger, hurt and disappointment will keep coming forth. If such emotions become too strong, then they can turn into hatred as well.

The course of true love never did run smooth.

—WILLIAM SHAKESPEARE. *(2008), A MIDSUMMER NIGHT'S DREAM*

If the twin soul is 'blind', then they cannot make an effort to come out of it, but if they are awake and feeling such hatred, they should make an effort to clear their negative energies. They should slowly shift to a better vibration than being caught up in a wave of hatred; harbouring such energies can turn out to be more harmful to themselves more than anyone else.

You might think that if your twin is with you, you would have the same feeling, but if a barrier within still exists, you will not be able to feel the love.

Think of it like this, your twin might know love and have an idea of it based upon what they have experienced in this world. Then you come along, and they can't explain the feeling, and it's almost too powerful and consuming.

They can get frustrated by the effect of this and project what they are feeling on to you. They might not understand why they are thinking of you all the time and why they keep being drawn back to you. It can be somewhat unsettling and expose their vulnerabilities. Accordingly, lashing out at you for no apparent reason or ignoring you or indulging in outright bad behaviour opposite of what they are actually feeling is not uncommon.

Don't worry about your twin both loving and hating you. You might worry if they feel nothing at all; indifference is love's kryptonite.

Forgiveness has the power to free you and help you move on and effectively get you to the harmony and the union you desire.

Twin flame connections often entail wounds and hurt that can be very challenging to let go, and understandably so; forgiveness is not always so easy in practice. So if you're finding it a little bit hard to forgive or let go of the hurt, there's nothing wrong with that.

Sometimes we equate forgiveness with weakness; we think that forgiveness makes us weak, that it means giving up our power and entails letting someone treat us as their doormat.

Forgiveness is actually something that frees you from negativity; forgiveness means taking back your true power. It enables you to let go of attachments and hurts that have been holding you back.

When you're staying attached to the situation that hurt you, you are actually holding inside of you those feelings of hurt, and that resentment towards your twin over time becomes a side of you, an impasse you can't get by that creates a blockage on your journey.

So in effect, many twins are contributing to their own separation by feeding old wounds and hanging on to negativity.

Forgiveness helps to release negativity, raise our vibration, heal wounds, release old attachments, increase unconditional love, and is one of the most important things we can do on this journey.

Fear is usually tangled up with guilt and shame, one of the lowest, heaviest energies of the spectrum, so in order to form and open new bonds from a place of pure unconditional love, forgiveness is essential.

Forgiving isn't a one-time action; it's something we do over and over on our journey, and it gets easier and more enjoyable each time.

Love is about harmony and unity. We cannot have harmony where there is blame, judgement and resentment, so forgiveness is an essential tool on the spiritual path. It helps us let go of pain patterns and open up to a state of love both inside and outside.

The twin flame connection is a journey we must attain as human beings, the balance we naturally had as souls, to be in harmony no matter how unequal the situation has been before. That's where the connection of love lies.

Buddhism understands and explains very clearly that as long as we hold on to events and people with our energy and emotions, and attachments, we are trapped, and it becomes hard to transcend into higher vibrations.

The twin flame union process is all about purification of energies to return to the same core frequency or soul song we share, so one of the most important things that can move us forward towards the union is forgiveness.

If you ever feel like giving up, try this one last thing to forgive both yourself and the other person in this situation. You don't have to forget, just release the grip on pain; when you forgive you allow the negative energy to leave. If you hold on to the hurt, you're calling in for more and more pain. By forgiving you remove the tension that was pulling the two of you apart into a repetitive cycle of conflict and problems, and you help them feel safe to open up again. And if you find it hard to forgive, it is understandable.

But when you do forgive them, when you approach them with unconditional love, you change the playing field entirely.

You are not allowing a negative behaviour; you're simply releasing it, so that it's not in your space hurting you anymore. You are not weak to forgive; in fact, you are strong enough to take care of yourself by releasing the hurt rooted in your feelings of shame or anger for allowing another person to mistreat you. So forgive yourself too.

Being open to a new idea can help; remember that behind the facade, your partner might be hurt because they have been playing pretend and been denying their true feelings for years. Show them that you're accepting of men having strong feelings or that you perceive strength to be more than just muscles and money.

Many divine feminines cling desperately to the dream of a physical union without realising this is the very thing keeping them apart from what they most desire.

To keep trusting the signs you have gotten, to keep believing your inner guidance when in the heart of your pain and reality is such a far cry away from the outcome you dreamt. An illusion fuelled by the idea of having found the ultimate partner that keeps us going through all the pain and despair. Until we reach a point where we can navigate on our own until we realise that there is so much more we did not see or understand before, and our life transforms in ways beyond our imagination.

Then you lose your grip and let them run far and wide because every road will eventually lead them back to you. No matter the miles or distance crossed when you finally stumble and realise the most obvious thing of all, that your feet and tears have passed the same ground, you left the loss and gain of all things, and now you get to feel the love, there was no separation. For centuries, the world has been focused on non-forgiveness, holding on to resentment and conflict. Just take a look back into history. On the twin flame journey, our core beliefs on what it means to be a strong and admirable person are subconsciously sabotaging our efforts to forgive and to let go of the very thing that is bringing us pain. Many people have a subconscious belief that causes a lot of resistance in the face of forgiveness.

If there are people in your life who push your buttons, then the only right path through that relationship is forgiveness without judgment, and if all of this fails and you still can't pass by the conflict then step away from them and away from the situation.

This can be difficult to swallow, but just know that not only love but also hate relationships are moving in the same direction as you are. They are moving with you, through your personal growth, and as you find wholeness, you become a master – you design your direction; you stop being a passenger and put yourself on the driver's seat in your life. A meaningful relationship comes out of love, not fear, so be mindful of how you're reacting to what is the dominant emotion – love or fear.

CHAPTER 15

It's Time to Be Clear

I'M A FIRM BELIEVER THAT every relationship can and should be happier than the last, and the only way you can have this is to learn from the experience. If you want to form deeper bonds, then you need to identify the dating pattern you've been looped in and make a change.

When dealing with karma, we have two options. We go through it by opening our hearts and minds, leaving the pain and disappointment behind, or we close up and feel betrayed and disappointed, attract a similar relationship, are hurt again, and the cycle repeats.

This means that the lesson wasn't learned, and the wisdom this situation holds is strongly resisted by you, but as soon as the wisdom is accepted by you, you get a flash of clarity, and the problem dissolves by itself without any logical explanation.

Everything in the universe seeks balance and stability, so when you figure out what karma teaches you and start letting go, the force has no opposite energy to keep this particular lesson in your life. Karma is released, and its purpose fulfilled.

Returning to your path requires a change of course with the people and situations you surround yourself with, and karma is your compass.

Ignore it, and it will only get harder and harder; follow it and learn from it, and pain will gently fade away. If it doesn't feel right, then learn to look at it with new eyes and in a different way; learn to follow 'that' with the actions that support it.

Think of going through life as driving a car; you follow the roads that lead you to your desired destination, avoiding turnarounds that would move you further away. This is a key fundamental practice for co-creating strong spiritual relationships.

Your earlier thoughts, feelings, patterns, energies, actions have all been part of creating this now moment and what you're currently experiencing. So, in each now moment, make sure you choose what will lead to your ideal.

It's only when we try to figure it all out with our minds that it's difficult. The easiest and best way is to sense the feeling of what we interact with. When both twins are telepathically and energetically connected on the heart chakra, they would get a deep sense of knowing, between themselves. Strong emotions can be felt, whether positive or negative, and the two of you will experience excessive emotions – positive during exciting moments, intensively low during sad moments. As the universe brews your tea, you will realise that subconsciously you have been running away from all your inner turmoil. The only way to overcome your trials and tribulations is to face them head-on.

But karma won't just take you from one day to another, from dim-wit to Einstein; the order in which the lessons come is the order in which your soul is learning. Karma isn't about good or bad luck as some refer to it; it's not some kind of magical punishment or suffering. It's simply the most perfect circumstances for someone to learn a particular lesson.

This kind of energetic connection usually has a well-defined purpose, and that is to remind us of the old wounds we carried from past lives, but no matter what, they aren't meant to last.

One of the hardest things to do is to let go; break-up is never easy. We fight to hold on to even the tiniest grain of hope, and we fight to let go.

The desire to have a relationship triumph comes because the attraction and experience can be very powerful, and who wouldn't want it to succeed? If we start looking at karma truthfully, patterns begin to emerge; then our conscious understanding moves beyond a certain point and we can no longer go back to our old understanding.

As karma function balancing, we often meet karmic partners who are meant to show us how far out of balance our life is.

When your love is unrequited in a karmic relationship, the worst thing to do is to not let go. If you hold on to this person for too long, this just prevents you from moving forward to newer possibilities of happiness. People who don't let go on time out of fear of being alone or never finding someone, end up marrying their karmic partners, live in frustration, in a pool of sadness, and mostly end up in divorce.

Ego plays a huge role in understanding karma; most of the dark karma comes from an unchecked ego and dysfunctional pride. Such relationships have a very limited shelf life and are very limited and loaded with sticky conditions.

If, for some reason, interactions are no longer productive, and no matter how much you try you just don't seem to find common ground, then maybe it is time to change course with that person; it's time to clarify your thoughts. When you have a personality clash and you just can't seem to get past it, or no matter what terrible thing was said or done you keep going back for some more, this attraction is designed by karma to keep you still with that person, so that the karmic lesson can unfold. Just walking out of the door, leaving the situation without clarifying things, not leaving the old baggage of the past relationship behind where it belongs, will land you right back in the same situation again.

Sometimes you might think you are over them, but the second they contact you, you drop everything and run straight to them, accept their stupid excuses even if you know how foolish that is, but you are happy as long as they want you for that moment.

You may also suppose that one day they will change, but this is something that was established in the first week of meeting them, not after years of hurt and strain.

Sometimes we do go back because it's easier than arguing or the kids are missing them or you feel you don't have a choice, but then you have to start the whole process all over again, with an entire range of new hurt feelings. There will be so many circumstances in which you will need to see them, especially where children are involved, and floods of memories come flashing back. Time does heal all wounds, but you can't live in the good memories of the past; the past is never going to come back.

So when do you know it's over? The very moment that you declare your relationship is a disaster is the moment that you need to back off and look carefully at how you got there. Blaming the other person for your mistakes is an emotional cop-out that just leads you to darker karma. In order to avoid a disaster and save the relationship, you need to look closely at the dysfunction of your own ego.

When the relationship is no longer productive, when it's all about them, when your feelings don't matter and you become their emotional doormat, when you've extended your personal tolerance as far as you can and the issue is still unresolved, then you own the freedom to step away from them. It would be an opportunity to learn something new about yourself and overcome and look at life in a different way.

Anytime there is something in your way that can't be avoided, and you have to go through the experience, it is karmic.

See yourself as a stone. If it is an unavoidable situation, then simply become a stone and be present for the lesson; slow down and let the lesson change you, even if it's just a little bit. If Mother Nature decides to hail on you, freeze. If you try to roll over and get away, just to become bitter about it afterwards, you haven't completed the lesson.

A simple way to understand this is to see it as a classroom where karma is both the teacher and the lesson. Show up in class, pay attention to the experience, do your inner work, conquer your fears and emotions, and that will make you feel empowered in your own strength. Karma is taking you back to school so that you can move your life forward, and it's entirely up to you if you pass or come back later to repeat it, go to class, learn the lesson and pass it by facing the unsettled emotions expressed as you find yourself in your own dark corner.

Karma holds you against your will to the wall so you can't move, forcing you to look at your issues. It gives you no choice but to face it, and the very moment you see the illusion in it, it sets you free, and you get your power back. Moreover, from there you will find new relationships with new lessons and new opportunities for growth, each experience moving you towards wholeness and freeing you from the drama of karma.

Walking on eggshells and not being free to be yourself is the opposite of being authentic, which is not about being a bully and having everything your way. It's about having space and freedom to breathe, or liberty for self-expression.

If healing does not take place in a twin, it may be because they have not been given the freedom to be who they really are in this world; this is something the other twin will provide; thus running begins.

Here is the thing though — karma doesn't differentiate between you and someone else. It sees all that you do to another, the same as you are doing to yourself.

An egoless relationship is one in which you are constantly aware of the ownership and responsibility of your own emotional ego, because trust is *that* without question. You choose love over fear, no walls, no bars, no looks or pointing fingers, no miscommunication, everything you feel is yours, everything they feel is theirs. Ending a karmic relationship means you will connect more to you, because only you can truly see yourself, and only you can actually know what you need. When you put the responsibility on someone to provide for you what you need, drama will be the result. Acting from your own personal perspective is empowerment, knowing the direction of your life. Be with someone because they are fun to be with, not because they complete you; only you can complete yourself.

Take back your inner power, stand up for yourself, identify dysfunctional behaviours in others and don't engage with them. When you start to see along those lines, see faults in others, then you will be able to see it in yourself as well. Set up high standards within yourself to have a high quality of life and only allow those who nurture and support this quality to come into your inner circle. Standing strong in your own convictions, without pushing those ideas onto someone else is a declaration for the self by the self. This is self-empowerment.

> *I believe that a simple and unassuming manner of life is*
> *best for everyone, best for both the body and the mind.*

—Albert Einstein (2013), The Ultimate Quotable Einstein

Illusion is always made to be a difficult path to follow, and truth is always made to be easy. It's always your choice to ignore the messages of a karmic relationship; ignorance is bliss. However, the truth is that the more aware and conscious you become of the mess, the less easy it will be to ignore the actions that must follow. So with those standards, you navigate through your relationships. There is nobody out there that can who has the authority to know whether you have met your Twin, except for you; only you know what it is that you need; the other people are only guessing.

When you postpone this growth, the longer you leave it, the harder it gets. But there is no easy way out, and this has to begin with you. Release the past, all the doubts about yourself, and start afresh; reinvent yourself and get your power back. As you do so, don't pay heed to the put-downs you may receive from those who sense the change. The dark energy is lurking in them, as they experience fear of losing you; they are threatened by your light. It won't be easy, but it will be better than to live with them. You may go through a hard time after a split. Your children, your family and your ex may persist in making you pay for mistakes, but still you must push forward. Even after you have come out of these entanglements, you may still get angry or go back to your old ways of thinking, but you would have made an important discovery. You will find out that you made it after all, and you can't believe how you could have stayed there all that while. If you are in a circumstance like this and you are not sure how to get out, or if you don't want this person to harass you, then you need to be certain that you are ready to leave and there is no way you will be going back.

In the world of love, there is no 'me and I'; there is only 'we and us'. Come in alignment with yourself, that precious gift that you are, and when both of you see the light in each other, then you have a match. When you see and connect, you are empowered with the light of truth, and you raise the vibrational frequency that you are in. See it as a spinning disk; the faster it is spinning, the less will stick to it, karma being the mud that wants to stick to it. The more aware you are, the shorter the journey becomes into finding your way back home. When we do, we can move on to relationships that inspire us to grow through self-reflection rather than demand that we grow through conflict.

Remember that room full of people we were talking about at the beginning. Visualising yourself there again, you can tell if you've moved on. You are over them when they are no longer in your conversations. When every other person doesn't remind you of them, when you see them and look into their eyes and feel nothing, that's when you know you are completely freed and you are moving on.

Energy cleansing is really like a shower. It's like you never washed before and then one day you go under that hot water and let it wash away all the dirt, the sweat, the past. A few hundred years ago no one brushed their teeth, but now we can't even imagine a day going by without doing it.

Whether we are with a karmic partner whose only purpose is to come into your life to be a catalyst, or if they are the soulmate whose here to challenge us to become the best person we can be, simply put, if they are our other half, this is no love that we have to beg for, enslave ourselves to or hold on tightly to out of fear of losing it.

You don't need to fix them, they need to fix and heal themselves.

So now you wait; patience is key, but that does not mean sitting around waiting for them. This is because if it turns into that, what it really implies is that you need them to be whole, and the idea is to become whole on your own without anyone else.

Honour the people who stir things up, honour the ones who don't; they are all your ultimate teachers. Every next level of this game called life will demand a new you. Love with all you've got.

CHAPTER 16

Stranger's Eyes

*Until my soul connected with yours, how could
I have known I was always in search of you?*

—BLACKBIRD

IN OUR SOCIETY, IT IS very common to hear the word 'soulmate'. Almost everyone who has fallen in love has called the object of their affection their soulmate. But is it really that simple? If everyone we fall in love with is a soulmate connection, then how can we know who is the 'one'?

For far too long we have been seeking for a soulmate we thought was the 'one' who can heal us, that person we can finally have a happy life with. The truth is, there are plenty of soulmates and karmic relationships out there, but there is only 'one' person who can offer you that once-in-a-lifetime type of love, and that is your twin.

It looks like there is much confusion in the spiritual community about the possibility of having more than one half for your soul. A perfect divine mirror of us is already confusing enough, why it would be another one? This would only make things more complicated and the journey more difficult than it already is. What makes this even more complicated is that many of those so-called experts who are writing about these concepts do so from a place of their own wounding.

Many people are stuck in relationships that are actually very unhealthy, and they are keeping themselves from evolving. This seems to result in a large part of the so-called experts saying unrequited love, co-pendency, pain, third-party situations and other toxic behaviour are all twin flame union signs.

Many mistake universal signs of deep soul recognition and synchronicities to indicate a twin flame. People are putting their lives on hold, spending far too much time and energy focusing on their partner and trying to understand their behaviour rather than focusing on themselves and relationships that could help them evolve.

A twin flame experience is your ultimate soul truth; it is something you must experience and realise, not verify through objective signs.

Many of us suffer from a significant lack of self-love, and sometimes this deficiency leads us to love obsession, desperately seeking love outside of self – most of the time because we weren't taught how we could be a source of love itself.

Not everyone came into this world to find a kind, loving, supportive family, and because of this, dysfunctional behaviour patterns emerge and can have us behave in detrimental ways.

So those who write from a wounded state do not possess the emotional resources to show up in life in fine fettle.

Many of us are holding on to people who only came into our life for a reason or for a season, believing or hoping they are the 'one', but it doesn't quite work like that. This odyssey is not about getting back with your partner; it is not about changing yourself beyond recognition just to not lose someone's love; it is not about flipping yourself backwards in order to keep someone in your life. That is co-dependency.

It does not mean that in order to unite with your twin flame you must transform yourself into an archetype of the divine feminine and masculine, some sort of mother of saints and the Messiah.

Because the truth is that unconditional love isn't found in perfection, part of the challenge and gift of the twin flame is to unconditionally love as *humans*.

These so-called false twins are just karmic partners who vibrate at the same frequencies as the partner they are attracted to, but the thing is, your soul will know. When you meet your twin flame, there is no doubt in your mind, body or soul that this is indeed something special, hard to explain in words. Only time will show if this person your heart belongs to is indeed your twin flame, but many people are impatient to stick on a label to this connection, which leads to a lot of disorientation.

Knowing whether or not somebody is truly your twin flame is something that takes quite some time. You need to truly believe it and know it. Twin flames can push and pull each other and bounce in and out of each other's lives for years. But if many years later you find that you still keep coming back to each other, and that the love and passion is still there just as strong as ever, then there's a strong possibility that it is a twin flame relationship and not just an obsession or a soulmate relationship meant to be in your life for a short time and then end. Again, keep in mind that this could also happen with other love relationships if you have a social contract with them that dictates this.

If this wannabe twin uses your wounds and weaknesses against you to make you run after them in a game that will never end, if this narcissistic partner gives you crumbs just to keep your hope alive, while you are subject to numerous betrayals and transgressions, then the person whom you are chasing is nothing more than a void, an empty mask with nothing underneath.

If they are holding you back from your dreams, goals and aspirations, if they are demeaning and undermining you so that they don't lose their grip on you, then that person is not your twin.

If no matter what they do, you can't help but go back for more impossible conflicts, where things are never really resolved and they are just swept under the rug, then if you want to make progress on your path to achieve your dreams, you'll eventually have to leave them and go at some point. This relationship can only be used as a catalyst to purge you back into your path. Remaining in this relationship beyond the expiration date will hinder you and your dreams; it will not help you. But the 'one', your one and only twin, will always provide you with the foundation and support for your mission, whatever that may be, and together you will be the ultimate power couple. When one is weak and powerless, the other will be strong, so your combined gifts and talents will be a strong force that can create massive change and influence.

Your true twin will give you such strength and make you feel as if anything and everything is possible. They will encourage you to achieve outstanding heights, climb new mountains and shoot for the moon. They are designed to be your perfect match, the person who will inspire and push you towards great personal growth.

The connection between you and your twin is a bond that both of you honour as sacred, whether it is platonic or romantic. Simply put, your existence is happier with them in it because you've both already done the inner work to heal before the final eclipse.

The karmic connection that you wrongly believe is your twin will look more like a real twin than your actual twin. They'll be identical to you, have the same interests, lifestyles and upbringing. On the other hand, your real twin flame will not be identical. You will be more like opposites, so you'll think this person can't be your twin as you don't have much in common. But that's because you're yin and yang, filling in what the other is missing.

Your twin will be present even when you're separated; it's impossible to shake them off. Your twin will have a very emotional way of connecting very deep that will cause the physical connection to be mind-blowing. It's something you would never have felt; you will lose yourself in their embrace. It'll be so intense, it'll be hard to even be around each other because every emotion is magnified, good or bad.

It'll be better if you're cautious about making the twin flame experience the end of all experiences of pure love. This is a rough road to travel, and it is just not everyone's destiny to walk on it, nor does it have to be.

Inner wounding might make you cling to this person, believing that your life and your happiness depend on it. The fact that you are obsessed with them and desperately want to hold on to this 'one' person, and not be able to let go can indicate a twin flame connection. But there isn't just the two of you involved in this journey; there are three: you, your twin and the divine. Only time will tell if you're together in this through thick and thin.

I truly believe that the universe will find a way to make sure you know without a shadow of a doubt that somebody is your twin flame and, however it may happen, it will be very specific and unique to you. However, this can still be a problem as with everything revolving around twin flame connections – what will happen to the individual you.

People want to believe that they are one of a kind, and they want their relationship to be special and unique, or they just want to try to justify why somebody did not want them and why they should move on and let go.

You really need to be honest with yourself whether or not you're just obsessing over somebody or you are imagining signs and synchronicities and messages from the universe.

Ask yourself if you just see what you want to see, and remember that on a subconscious level your mind will show you what you want to see.

The answer may not be clear-cut, and you might have to learn to take everything with a grain of salt. But if you keep an open mind and don't latch on to the idea of a twin flame so fast, you'll have a better chance of getting a clear and decisive answer from the universe to guide you, and a better chance of seeing what the universe is trying to show and tell you.

And keep in mind that this connection is believed to be incredibly rare, although, yes, we all have a t win there somewhere. One's twin incarnating at the same time, at any given time, in any given life is supposed to be very rare, or maybe they do but you aren't meant to catch up with each other in this particular life.

We will all go through our twin flame life cycles. Some believe there is set number of lives we are able to reincarnate with our twin; many believe we only have this life to find our other half; others think this cycle goes on and on until we achieve union. Nevertheless, whatever your belief, the first and last lives serve as a reminder of our twin existence in the flesh and the physical. The other lives tend to be all about karma. Those lives serve to help us grow and evolve; these experi-ences will always remain somewhere in our subconscious.

Now I said this is what is usually believed because, for all we know, it may be entirely possible for any twin flame connection you are in to be only a karmic life cycle together, just to go through karma and to raise a vibrational frequency in preparation for the union life cycle.It is said that we have already scheduled our meeting with our twin; before we are born into this life, we agreed on the timeline for bumping into each other.

You cannot just plan for a night out and find this kind of love. It will happen when you are ready, when the time is right, and there isn't any guarantee that you will actually meet them in this lifetime, and even if that happens, you may not unite and become 'one'.

But our last life on earth in the third dimension is said to be the one in which we unite, where the sun and moon finally come together into the eclipse. The life where you come together with your twin in a romantic and lasting union, after you have finished all the lessons and balanced all the karma required in your soul contract, is when you can have a successful relationship with your twin.

So there's a really good chance the majority of actual twins who have incarnated together are not in union lives; that's why there are so many sad, sob stories. Some sets of twins find themselves get stuck in a karmic life cycle and may not come together or stay in a lasting union in this lifetime, them along with the countless people who just assume or insist that they are in a twin flame relationship.

And though we are all twins, statistically at any given time, within any given life, your twin might be on the other side, may not have been born into this life with you yet or something unfortunate may have happened to them, and you don't get the chance to connect in this particular lifetime. This means that there's a really good chance that a vast majority of people who claim to be in a twin flame relationship are not.

It is difficult to know if you've been incarnated with your twin. So many people think so, and they attribute their experience with others to a twin soul connection even when there's a great chance that they are not incarnated with their twin.

We don't just incarnate with our twin flames for the purpose of the union; we do so for the purpose of clearing karma, balancing our energies and raising our vibration in preparation for the union life. In other words, there are two different types of life cycles with our twins, a karmic one and a union one.

So if you feel unloved, betrayed, abandoned, unfulfilled, angry, just to name a few ways you may feel, then you need to be honest about this situation and know that you deserve happiness on all levels.

Bringing karma to completion does not mean ending the relationship, or falling out of love with them; it means transforming your awareness and realising that the other person is not responsible for your happiness, you are. It involves converting your awareness and being more responsible with your own emotional balance, or the difference in action instead of reaction. For everything that you feel compassion for, you have already expressed and learned the value of the lesson.

Breaking up is never easy, because it can bring up a lot of buried emotions. The good news is that you can avoid a lot of this pain if you end things before resentment builds. If the relationship has already deteriorated past this point, it's only going to get worse the longer you wait. There are no perfect breakups. Keep what you say short and respectful and then give your former partner space to process.

Pure devotion does not need to say it's loyal; if you need to tell someone that you're going to be loyal then you're coming from a place of hesitation. Devotion as pure as it is, is still karma; if you sacrifice yourself for the devotion of others, you create self-karma – that's what the imbalance of giving to others and giving to yourself looks like.

Give yourself plenty of alone time to reflect. The worst thing you can do is to move on too quickly.

The karmic relationship you just got out of is full of lessons that, if you can learn from them, will help you choose a more compatible partner. Identifying which parts of the relationship made you stronger will help you accept the experience as a whole.

The person who does not want a relationship with you but just wants you for the good times or only when it pleases them will sometimes be the hardest to let go off. They will show you a loving side you are longing for, and so you believe they are almost perfect, that they are the 'one'.

A major lesson for us is that we just have to learn to be strong enough to let them go and move on when the time comes, because no matter what type of relationship we have, we shouldn't have to chain ourselves to it in order not to lose it.

One thing is clear: if you have a strong attraction to someone and you know they are not right for you, yet you keep visualising yourself as happy with them, it can be one of the most confusing things to try to get out of.

It goes without saying that there is a thin line between connection and obsession; someone can use the concept of twin flames unwisely to justify not being able to accept the end of a breakup or even to extend an unhealthy relationship that might even be abusive. Most of the time, twin flames come into our lives to teach us an invaluable lesson.

Of course, when you see the person you love with someone else it breaks you, but love isn't just about the emotions you have. It's also about what this person means to you; it's about their place in your life as well as your heart. When you realise your loved one is with someone else, you see the life you thought you'd have disappear, as it is no longer possible.

You'll be a different person than you were an hour ago; you will no longer feel and see the things the same way. Your life has just changed.

The part of you that was left behind gives room for growth; it's a blank sleeve, an opportunity to rewrite and redefine the person that you are.

If you honestly want the deepest love you can have in this world, then you won't find it behind closed doors with somebody who is not your twin. Because the greatest love story ever, though, is the one you can have only with your beloved twin, the other half of your soul.

CHAPTER 17

Shadow of a Dream

TWIN SOULS HAVE TO FIND their way back, to be one again, but this time as 'one' soul in two bodies.

For those who cross paths with their twin and have the chance to meet them, the best is to be in a relationship with them, as it stimulates personal growth in a way they have never experienced before.

Love is the reason why twin flames choose to separate from each other and find their way back together.

There can be no darkness in a union which is made purely of light; the road is tough and must be walked alone, but it is truly for your highest good.

All twin flames are ultimately on the journey back to each other and to union in some way or other. For some it's direct and smooth, for others it winds back and around itself. Remember, as always, that each twin journey is unique and individual because we all have different karmic baggage and energetic backgrounds with varying experiences.

It may feel like your twin has abandoned you; physically the journey of separation is walked alone, but in spirit, you always walk side by side.

Twin flame souls are drawn to one another; they call out to one another like the flame calls to the moth or like lightning calls to the thunder, and you find each other in every single lifetime.

Dare you follow your endeavours, you will suffer, but the beauty, passion and love, in the end, will make it all worthwhile.

If one or both of you were never stirred to work on personal growth, to begin with, your meeting would not change much, and you won't fulfil your mission. However, the opportunity for progress will always be there. But we cannot make someone learn a lesson that they are not ready for. Despite the development of each twin or lack thereof, the potential for achieving union will always be there. But this does not guarantee a happily ever after in this lifetime. If both twins have not attained their soul potential and matured, no matter how much they love one another, a union in this lifetime will not be possible.

What is so surprising and contradictory at the same time is how bounded but also free your twin flame makes you feel when they are around. You are free to be yourself, free to express all your deepest emotions, have the freedom to feel free at the core but yet feel an unbreakable connection with them; you're like a fish out of water when they are not around.

There is no wrong about this journey, so be gentle with yourself and stay open to the process unfolding in what might potentially be unexpected ways. You are here now for a reason, and here and now is where your journey is revealing itself.

You are not powerless in the unfolding path of your spiritual love connection; you define your own journey more than you might have ever realised. You choose; you are the designer of your own destiny and your experience.

Make sure you let go of the unconscious material that has kept you focused on other people, on society, and kept you locked to playing life by the rules.

And when you embrace the wild adventures that await you, take you into the ultimate heights of love beyond what you've ever experienced, it truly can become an experience where you feel love with every breath.

We are all here to experience unconditional love while still in physical existence; that is one of the twin flame missions.

The truth is, all twin flame journeys are about love, but twin sets each choose from a variety of lessons and paths and ways to journey into a life that will bring them back to the unity that existed between them once.

In New Age spirituality, some spiritualists are under the impression that twin flames are identical and that there is a rule book lying out there for every move that you must make to reach that happy place and unity you're longing for.

The honest truth is that you are the key to your happy union; your uniqueness is not just an interesting facet of your life experience.

Your personality and early life experience were deliberately chosen by you to manifest the kind of blessings and challenges you desire. Your life experiences plus who you are as a soul contains all the ingredients you need to unite in a happy state of unconditional love. On your journey, your soul carries key signs of the particular path to love that you and your twin uniquely chose to focus on. Some twins might decide to harmonise age difference, to change religious beliefs, to crash cultural bridges and to open people's eyes to gender differences.

> *Nor when love is of this disinterested sort is there any disgrace in being deceived, but in every other case, there is an equal disgrace in being or not being deceived. For he who is gracious to his lover under the*

> *impression that he is rich, and is disappointed of his gains because he turns out to be poor, is disgraced all the same: for he has done his best to show that he would give himself up to any one's 'uses base' for the sake of money; but this is not honourable. And on the same principle he who gives himself to a lover because he is a good man, and in the hope that he will be improved by his company, shows himself to be virtuous, even though the object of his affection turn out to be a villain, and to have no virtue; and if he is deceived he has committed a noble error. For he has proved that for his part he will do anything for anybody with a view to virtue and improvement, than which there can be nothing nobler.*
>
> —Plato (2016), Symposium

But keep love in your heart and keep the faith. Send them unconditional love. It is just part of the ride; you can't control the process. Your soul will love this; the challenge makes you grow on a soul level. Your soul knows there are many lessons along the way, and even when you can't understand the theory, actually feeling it and living it is a different matter when your ego is panicking and throwing a tantrum. The ego wants it all now; your soul knows it takes time to grow and remember who you actually are.

The ego would love a university degree on the twin flame connection, but the soul knows that is pointless; ultimately, it's all about love.

Begin to look for the light in everything and everyone, including yourself; the more you do this, the more it shines through, and the greater your capacity for giving and receiving love, the higher your vibration.

Separation doesn't mean you are unlovable; it is there to give us space to work on what we need to. Your ego won't see it like this. It will probably do everything to try and convince you that it won't work, you can't live without them, and so on. Learn to recognise when your ego is manipulating you; you can't make it die, but you can learn to identify when it is controlling you.

Separation is there to bring you back to love, to give you space. You are going through massive shifts, and you have to be able to make yourself happy first; happiness is an inside job. Try and find things that bring you pleasure, no matter how small. This can get very hard when you are in so much pain and that alone can't calm you, but accept where you are and concentrate on the small things. You might think you can't do it, but you can overcome this.

It is normal to feel distraught, unhappy and gravely wounded by a loss of this magnitude, but this seemingly cruel act is the universe's attempt to bring you closer to you and closer to oneness.

This is not the typical boy meets girl or man meets a woman story; it's a completely different ball game. In normal relationships, there is always doubt, the feelings are relative and they depend on the circumstances.

This is connection and devotion for each other that is so profound that the four-letter word love would never seem enough to explain it.

This spiritual connection is never just a regular relationship. Many struggle on this journey because they try to approach the connection with traditional relationship advice in mind.

It will always be a journey beyond normality when you can open up to the truth and realise that this journey can't be jammed into the old ideals of romance; you can genuinely allow this connection to blossom.

This spiritual connection never stops evolving, growing and transforming like all other connections do. When you end up embracing this perspective that what's ahead is bright, is for your highest good and is a learning opportunity, then you can enjoy the connection so much more than those who worry and end up stumped.

We need to allow ourselves and others equal love, and trust the universe; these are the great qualities that all twin flames have within. If you are in this predicament, then examine your motives and ask yourself if you are doing this coming from a place of love; if you do, then act on it.

We all know that love is always the most beautiful motivator. If this is not the cause of your inaction or action, then you may have to adjust your reasoning so that you may follow your greatest meaningful path.

Because the truth is that we are masters of only our own life, we do not have control over the rest of the universe, and we must be prepared for that.

We must decide whether to make a sacrifice or not. The harder this decision is, the more critical it might prove to be. For the soul that existed before we were born, this cannot have been an easy sacrifice to make. And through our lives, we experience many, many decisions that require us to make a sacrifice.

Everything is orchestrated by the universe, and the sooner you realise that the better it will get for you; instead of feeling sorry for yourself, take control.

You cannot be stuck in your own castle tower waiting for the rescue which may never come.

So you ultimately have only two options: stay in the usual mindset of what we think love looks like and try to fit this twin flame experience in there, which will just keep you hurt, stuck and entirely disempowered, even doubting your own sanity. Or you can shift your perspective and let this connection bring you where you are meant to be, fully fastened in a new perception of reality and in a much better place than where you were when you met your twin.

The journey can be full of magical synchronicities that help you find *that* something that you never even knew you were looking for.

But if you are always looking back, living in the past or looking into the future, how can you be here living now in this moment and enjoy the desired things that show up on your way?

You can't remain where you are and go where you're going.

CHAPTER 18

Walkabout

Create in me a pure heart and renew a right spirit within me.

—P<small>SALM</small> *51:10*

L<small>OOKING BACK ON OPPORTUNITIES YOU</small> missed won't help. It was all in your best interests even though you can't see it right now; in time when you get where you want, you will realise why events happened the way they did. So don't look back and regret anything. Look where you are now and ask yourself: Are you going to regret what you are doing now?

It's hard work, not for the fainthearted, and you have to face every part of you that you particularly do not want to look at. That is what the twin flame meeting does; it forces you to be brutally honest with yourself and be mindful for every ounce of inner wounding that still needs to be addressed.

There is also another area to read around and delve into. When processing emotional issues that you have no control over, don't get caught up in the story of it. You can choose to feel the experience of it without engaging in the expression of it. Like this, you burn any attachments to karma through the emotional charge and begin to express freedom from that issue, person or situation.

Grieving is important. Don't block it; feel it. Cry and let it flow through you without attaching any thoughts to it. Ask for it to be released. Release expectations - expectations are conditional love, and you are getting back into a state of unconditional love. You do this a bit at a time; it can be hard enough doing it bit by bit, but you simply cannot do it all in one go no matter how fast you would like it to go, and again this can take time and several trials even when you think you have cleared your way through an issue. Eventually, all that is left is love, and none of the bad stuff will rule you.

It is much more than chilling out on your yoga mat or doing meditation, drinking herbal tea and cleansing your aura; it's so much more than just doing all the right things and looking good while doing it. You won't be looking your best all the time, especially not when you are purging old emotions, while you are passing over the rocky part of this journey. Having to give answer to questions that, even when you answered them, no one really understands their meaning.

The problem with this advice is that not everyone is wired to be an optimist; not everyone is programmed to be able to go with the flow in relationships. Many carry karmic blockages and early life experiences that make us feel unsafe in opening up to love.

The human mind is constructed for survival, to keep us safe. This means forgiveness and unconditional love relationships stand low on its list of priorities. Opening up towards another person is considered extremely unsafe by the deeper wiring of the human brain.

Your optimal best is when you feel absolutely fantastic and tip-top in health and you are full of love, joy, energy and light. Huge enhancement of your abilities, not just creative but across the board, which is everybody's optimal best regardless of your connection, is what your soul and your cells in your body are crying for all the time. So when you go through this period of time when you are at your optimal best, you reach a state of complete peace. The union is not a mystical meditation or yogi state.

Your heart must feel like it has been through a shredder and you feel that you will most likely never feel happiness again. Once you are on this rollercoaster, there is no getting off; you are trying to shed the heavy, dense negative energies; relaxing when you don't actually have any control isn't easy.

The first is to give yourself lots of care, nurturing and the love you deserve yourself and not to look for anyone else to complete you but to love and accept yourself completely.

Do whatever puts you in a good mood; join a book club, go out for hikes in a group, make new friends, start new activities that you never tried, travel. Get out and about. Do self-affirmations; they will help you to get out of your low, or lowest points in life. The second most important thing to do is to get out of melodramatic thinking, so start being busy.

You will be amazed how such activities open up a new world. You will experience new things, and you will be forced to take on a new perspective, and as you do this, you will hardly get time to think about your twin. The work you do on yourself helps them too; you are strong enough. You won't possibly believe this right now, but you are.

Time heals, so it will come at a moment when you realise you have overcome the sadness, and you are living your life to the fullest. You will still love this person but not at the expense of your shortcomings or sadness; you will then realise what unconditional love is. Release yourself from this cycle and surrender. It will open so many new doors.

The more negativity there is surrounding you in the connection, the more signals you will receive that you have journeyed away from the path. The further you are from happiness and unity, the more you have been pulled down into old belief systems.

If there is hardship, suffering, frustration and hurt, it means the universe is trying to show you that you have journeyed away from the light, from oneness, from pure love.

The more you cleanse and release the old, the more you return to your soul's innocence, and the closer you return to purity and happiness, there will be no more judgements and perceptions.

I put a huge emphasis on energetic and emotional balancing, on emotional well-being. There is a simple truth to life: Guess how life is going to feel and look like to you, when you feel bad? Terrible indeed. It's really that simple; we need to get our act together on every level of our life. Twin flame journey is not just about the union; it is about finding balance in your life as well.

When we stay focused on the past, we keep recreating it; make sure you stay out of fear as it will only keep you attracting more of the same.

Detaching ourselves from judgement and releasing old beliefs and perceptions can help us invite in new joy, new solutions and new paths to love. It allows us to build a solid foundation and make sure anything causing instability gets removed to ground unconditional love into the physical realms.

Meditation is best for healing, but you also need to look at yourself to see why people hurt you so badly and what it was that you were putting out in the world.

Negative thinking brings bad things. Also, because we do not feel worthy, our minds create our lives, bad or good.

Meditation will give you answers and healing; it will heal your old pain and help you move past the ego, which is the hardest part.

The ego makes us do things and hurt people to still be in control of what we do. Heal, but also forgive what they did. Let go of the pain; if they are truly who you think they are, they will come back, so forgiveness is a must.

They need more time to learn to be with you, that's all, or maybe they are afraid of the connection and of losing control of who they are; sometimes they are not ready to be with you just yet.

The endless search for the lost twin will end when we realise it was really with us this whole time, just waiting patiently to be discovered. Now we get to realise that the person we once looked upon and loved beyond reason was our own reflection, and the light we once deemed ourself was our very own. Let your intuition guide you on your way, let it be your guiding light; our hearts are the only law of this universe.

Trust your gut; learning to listen to the voice of your heart, to your intuition, is key to a healthy spiritual relationship. The mind only knows the human rules for relationships; the heart knows we can be so much more. The mind cannot feel love, only the heart can. Listen to the wisdom your heart is sending you; it's always giving you signals of what's to come, what serves you and what doesn't. So listen to your heart, which is a loyal guide, an infallible compass.

You do not always need to seek insight by connecting to the higher realms and through mystical religious rituals, try instead to seek the divine connection within yourself, within your partner and within the sacred space between you.

Many people are so drawn in and overwhelmed by the intensity of their spiritual love connection that they lose hold of who they used to be. And although this is natural and understandable, it's important to be centred in your own uniqueness, your identity and passions, to be centred in self-love, both for yourself and for the sake of your connection.

Whether you are with your twin or not, know that they are always unconsciously mirroring back to you what you hold within.

Whenever you make someone accountable for your happiness, they feel pressured, and you're constantly in danger of losing your joy. There are several possible solutions you can try if you don't relish your life. With any negative situation in life, it can help to bear in mind that most lives aren't perfect.

It's possible for you to feel the truth and become aware of the way you've been living in an unnatural environment before that. You now no longer wish to stay that way; materialistic items may no longer matter to you.

There may be things you need to do, so you learn to love yourself first, release childhood hurt and social conditioning, learn to stand up for yourself and speak your mind, diet and exercise, recharge and lose unequal friendships.

The truth will gradually be known, and it's the truth that will set you free. For this reason, you've got to learn to move beyond your fears, and share what you desire. You need to understand how to control your emotions in a wholesome way.

To make a relationship work takes a lot of time and attention. Love and passion need nurturing and space to grow; all relationships need breathing space, time together and time with friends. Keep talking about what matters, pay attention to the things that don't work and continue to ask yourself what you can do that is positively different from yesterday.

When you feel like giving up, it's a sign that you're just about to experience breakthrough; the biggest shifts come after the biggest blocks have been confronted and moved. The biggest growth comes after the biggest push; often when you lose hope, the change you think may never happen is in fact around the corner. Every time we are upset and make a choice to forgive and love each other and put the past behind, our capacity to love grows and so will your love, which grows deeper and stronger and gets you and your twin flame closer to each other.

Everything that we think or do that is out of alignment needs to be balanced with forgiveness and compassion. Every thought, no matter how small, that is out of alignment, every emotion, every action is a payback called karma. Any space in your life that has been replaced by ego creates a shock wave of karma that disrupts the balance. We are put into situations with opportunities to experience and see life differently and choose how to respond to it. You always have the choice to resolve an issue by responding with forgiveness and cycle out of anger and back into compassion. Creating good karma comes from doing the right thing over the easy stuff and doing it for the right reason, and how that karma comes back to you is only up to you.

There's a shift that needs to happen, to turn the outside into the inside, to finally take on the monsters of your inner consciousness so that you can emerge into a new light, your twin true love, instead of trying to escape the darkness.

Transformation comes from within and from understanding what is truly going on in the non-verbal parts of our psyche confronting the shadows.

It is achieved by finding the places where we've lost ourselves, discovering where we keep ourselves locked into a self-made prison of thoughts and fears and finally opening the door because we realise that we had the key with us the whole time.

Embracing the shadow in us, shining the light of love on all the wounded parts of ourselves, that's the alchemy of self-love.

That's the biggest burden of the twin flame journey because it's not just about finding the man or woman of your dreams or being in love; it's about transforming the darkness within into light, using the power of love.

Make self-care a priority in your everyday life; you also have to accept where you are right now, while you continue to work on your shadow side and try to integrate it.

Like a true knight on a quest, you already know what awaits at the end – love. The love is already there; go into the darkness of your own psyche, confront the fears, the monsters of your mind.

Then the pain experienced would have not been for nothing. Use it to create profoundly moving work, and reach as many people as possible and contribute to shifting perspectives, on themselves, life, love, death, to transmute darkness into light.

Twin flames are like spiritual moths that used stars to guide themselves but instead got distracted by artificial light. It was too much for them, so they got lost.

You need to wake yourself and open up your eyes to the real light. Your heart is free; have the courage to follow it.

CHAPTER 19

Unconditional Love

And when one of them meets the other half, the actual half of himself, whether he be a lover of youth or a lover of another sort, the pair are lost in an amazement of love and friendship and intimacy and one will not be out of the other's sight, as I may say, even for a moment.

—Plato (2016), 'Symposium'

With twin flames, the love is unconditional, complicated and ill-fitting in this world. Understanding the power of it is a challenge.

Unconditional love is what sparks this twin flame dynamic; it is the driving force and the end goal.

One of the purposes of twin flame journey is to find unconditional love, which sounds great in theory, but

can become a problem when you cross a deeply wounded state of mind with a wish to find unconditional love.

We are highly empathic, and we have an incredible amount of wounding from both this life and other lifetimes that, in our attempt to show unconditional love, we become doormats.

This can involve feeling taken for granted, again and again, feeling angry at yourself for letting this happen, waiting around for your lost twin to the point of crossing your own boundaries. If it hurts you deeply, triggers deep wounds, keeps you small, makes you stop from moving forward, it isn't love. It's dysfunctional behaviour stemming from your deepest wounds, and it's also a karmic cycle.

Some twins get stuck in this pattern of dysfunctional behaviour for years, and sometimes decades, because they are attempting to have unconditional love without doing the necessary work.

The twin flame journey is an inside job; it's about getting really honest and looking at those sides of you that make you feel less-than; it's about looking at your decisions and the reasons why you accepted scraps of love, which is a sign of low self-worth. It is likely this has been a pattern throughout your life, and your twin is showing this to you so that you can break the cycle once and for all. He is holding you the mirror so that you can look at your reflection and see that this is not your true essence.

Remember you can only love another as deeply as you love yourself; this gets magnified when it comes to twin flames. You will find unconditional love in the twin flame journey as long as you have unconditional love towards yourself first.

When it's all said and done, you just know. But before that, you go on a bit of a trip of discovery.

We arrange to meet people who would be really hard to love, to remember why we're here because nice and loving people are easy to love. It's the ones who are hard to love who can show you the difference between conditional and unconditional love.

The reason for this is that hurt is a fantastic teacher; it breaks down the barriers we've built, shatters illusions and makes us remember who we really are; it makes us seek more, crave for more, pray for more. Hurt pushes us to the edge of what we'll tolerate; it makes us carry out changes and take risks and open up to what we might have otherwise been too comfortable or stuck to bother with.

If there is distance, it means there's negativity being stirred to the surface in your connection. In essence, if your twin is pulling away from you, it's because they haven't forgiven themselves; they feel bad about the past, they are picking up on collective negativity about this and holding themselves hostage with it, feeling like they don't deserve love.

Because when you're in love with who you are at your core, when you cherish and respect the person you have become, when your heart is overflowing with love, this is when you change the whole vibration of everything around you.

Unconditional love is the purest form of love, as it bears no attachments or conditions; it's the highest spiritual love you can achieve, and the path to discovering it is guided by the universe.

To love is to be able to give the utmost care to the object of your affection. It can be a person, a passion or a principle. To be so dedicated to your cause that you will leave no stone unturned to take care of it. Sometimes you will have to fight the world, sometimes your own self. Sometimes you will have to fight the object of your affection for his or her welfare. It might break you down or shatter your world, but when you truly love someone, you go beyond the optimum and take the trouble of going far beyond your limits. Because when you are in love, you are not concerned about justice or fairness; you are concerned about doing good.

It can be observed that people who've never learnt from their mistakes, who never changed and who grew from negative to miserable and remained that way are people who have never truly loved and probably never came in contact with real love. They don't seem to know what it means to truly be in love with someone, and it's like they don't even seem to care.

Thus, we who have come to this earth to love are the ones who are also expected to reach our highest potential, and then help others to heal.

If you are a person who has grown to know unconditional love, it means you came here with a great ability to love, and you are a noble soul expected to heal, grow and become whole. Twin Flame union brings so much love into this world, as we finally understand our own worth and divine origins. You've been given all the tools you need to do that; you know you were born for more than what the world is telling you is possible. In a way that is dificult to understand. The dark side of human nature is a benefit to the twins; in that, these challenges make the soul wiser, stronger and kinder.

It can be hard to admit that we ourselves as souls can arrange for hardship and challenges to occur in our lives. The very people who are rattling us the most are those who are reflecting back to us our own issues and wounds, and they are ultimately the ones who help us the most. Because they make us look deeper, they trigger us. If you want to make this pilgrimage smoother, to show your soul you're ready to move on from those hard knocks, start looking for the light inside everyone you encounter. Look for the child inside, the soul in them, the wounded person inside; look behind the facade. When you begin seeing this, you'll start to open up to unconditional love. True love that stretches beyond actions and words and behaviour.

Being with someone who doesn't seem to understand and see you is a relationship designed just for you, to heal and overcome this issue. Take this precious love you feel for someone who doesn't see you, and give it to yourself instead.

Karma teaches you how to heal from pain and suffering and hope for something better. When you do your inner work, and learn to respond with love instead of fear, karma gets cured; it becomes *that* without attachments, *that* without conditions for love, *that* of a guiltless mind. All this requires firm boundaries and a strong sense of self-value because karma will show you how much of a mess it can make when you don't practice healthy boundaries or feel good about yourself.

Listen to the voice of your soul, and remember the reason why you came down as one soul in the first place: for love.

You can heal and become who you are, who you came here to be, with or without meeting your twin flame. The journey of healing and becoming is not exclusive or framed by the context of a twin flame love. Obviously, if you've met your twin, it'll change you, boost you, speed you up and transform the way you go about your healing and becoming.

It means to accept all the hurt, to accept everything bad that's happened to you; it means to pick up from the floor all the pieces of ourselves and glue them back together, healing every pain with love.

That is when you will be able to bring out the love and connection with your twin flame; it will ignite the fire between you and the mirror to shine a bright reflection of love back to you.

If they are in your life and you know they are the 'one', then the universe has given you what you need, whether you are ready or not.

Twin flames enhance our life; they teach us lessons, whether it is about love or progression of life. They bring us what we may not have.

The point of this journey through hurt is to get you to question and release your perceptions, your beliefs and your self-limits, so you can ultimately love yourself and your twin unconditionally.

You are here to stand in your own power and be complete in yourself and move forward, and if your soul path is to connect with your twin again, then that will happen. But it will not happen when you wait for them to come, and if it's meant to come to play then it will come to you; the more you chase, the more they run.

Even if your twin is committed to someone else, you can still express your love without hesitation, but don't invade their personal life or force their hand. Give them space and time to make their own decisions; wait and let things run their course. You can reach into your core where love resides, the soul I mean, where you have and hold that feeling of unconditional love for everyone. This includes your twin flame; if you learn to release the negative and pent-up frustration, you throw yourself up at them and just open your heart and close your logical thinking mind and let this love well up in you to the point where it overflows; and you become this love energy that is irresistible to all, including your twin. You realise that your twin and you both have faults and will do things to tick each other off, but it isn't intentional.

You're just trying to get past all this rubbish to a place where, no matter what, all that matters in your lives is that you know you can get through anything because of your unconditional, non-judgmental love for them.

This comes from your soul and theirs. It does exist there and it did before you came to this earth. You've just forgotten this because of all the other things you've chosen to experience.

So learn to stop judging and blaming yourself for all the wrongs in your life, all the bad experiences, once you realise that you asked for most of them to come into your life to teach you more about yourself and how to be a better person.

One cannot love someone unconditionally while judging them and blaming them. One cannot be happy with others while being unhappy with oneself.

One cannot bring good to others without having gratitude in one's life for what one has and how far one has come.

One cannot accept another and their flaws and foibles without being able to do the same for oneself. This includes your twin flame. This is what you must do in order to love your runner twin unconditionally.

Heal yourself first, wait and see, let that love fill you up completely; even if it overflows it has nowhere to go but to your twin. They will then feel the love and be pulled towards you because no one else in the world can provide that pure love that flows from you to them. It is unparalleled, and the greatest thing you'll ever learn is to love and be loved in return.

When the pain that consumes you wanes, but you still feel your twin, you still feel love for them while wishing them nothing but happiness, know that you have achieved unconditional love.

CHAPTER 20

Born to Run

THE UNIVERSE BOUND YOU AND your twin in eternity before reincarnating in this world, long after any other earthly contract did; that is why the infinity sign is a holy symbol of twin flame love.

Meeting your twin does mean this is a very significant lifetime for you both; one of the main aims is for you to reconnect and hopefully try to unite once more in the divine sacred marriage of the souls, *hieros gamos*.

The term is used generally to refer to the sacred marriage between two divinities or gods, or between a human being and a god or between two human beings, under certain special conditions where the ultimate alchemy of forces harmonises polar opposites.

However, being forever in a love relationship with your twin isn't its only purpose; it's the ultimate push to expand our consciousness and discover our higher purpose.

A common manifestation of a twin flame connection is that both souls may have a keen interest in offering help to others or serving humanity in some profound way. It's very typical for them to resonate with similar or identical social causes and humanitarian issues in the world. Twin flames can also experience memories of past lives together or have visions of their mission together on the planet.

Twin flames frequently share similar important beliefs and positive morals and values deep down, even if it is not obvious on the surface of the personality, sometimes due to ego issues. There is an energetic polarisation between twin flames that can be complimentary as well – each may have characteristics and aspects of personality and interests and talents that are contradictory yet complementary.

Twin souls can usually have the most profound and heartfelt conversations that can even last for hours at a time. The heightened energy between twin flames can spark the most creative and imaginative ideas between them and can be just as profound if there is any arguing or disagreement about anything.

You can have an immense enhancement in your own creative abilities and, sometimes, psychic abilities as twin flames are here to help with the creative endeavours of humanity. Creative energy resides in the heart, so when the heart fires up, potential fires up.

Your twin flame mirrors your needs, desires, concerns, ambitions, dreams and hopes about those things that matter in your life. The two will also complement each other's skill sets and talents, to make each other truly complete.

But karmic partnerships can also motivate us to take better care of ourselves, understand ourselves and unleash our gifts and talents.

Twin flames will each embody their own unique traits, interests, passions and talents that will help them carry out their soul mission on earth, either apart or as shared purpose they may have together as a couple.

Because this ignition is never about just the two of you, it's never just about what you two want and need; it's always about the bigger picture. And the bigger picture is that twin flames are here for a purpose, a humanitarian mission, to clear the bloodlines of families or as a template for new divine partnerships. They are here to help society heal ancient wounds; to take on karmic baggage; to absorb hurt, conflict and limitations that humanity has experienced throughout history; to help us awaken to our true nature and unite in love; to heal karmic pain in key families and groups and to activate and gift the world, so the soul isn't particularly concerned about the dynamics that you have set up previously to the point where you have meet. If we go back in history, marriage is a man-made contract, a piece of paper made at a certain point in time to bind two people together for the rest of their lives.

When people get married, it is not that they are not connected to their partners in profound love from the soul and that it is not a beautiful connection; we cannot say this is not love, because I am absolutely sure it is. But if your twin comes in, it's an entirely different level of love and connection driven by the soul and the heart.

When twin flames marry, it is divine alchemy, a merging of souls, much more meaningful than any piece of paper. No man-made contract can ever take away from the connection, the alchemy and the sacred marriage bond between twin flames.

At one time, ages ago, humanity experienced this directly. Humans walked amongst the gods, talked with God, and could see the Heavens. This is symbolised in different ways in each religion and in the Bible in the man and woman in the Garden of Eden before the fall. And throughout the ages, the 'eternal lovers' have been known by various other names such as yab-yum in Tibetan Buddhism, the sacred marriage in the Kabbalah and, in some ways, tantra in Hinduism.

Probably the best-known historical example of the sacred union between twin flames is that between King Solomon and the queen of Sheba. Once she heard of King Solomon, she was moved by the very mention of his name, so she travelled far from her homeland to see him. Upon meeting one another, it is said that Solomon met his match and so did she; 'he took her breath away', but both knew they were special, despite the fact that they could never marry as they were rulers of different lands, and in those times you could marry only within your own kingdom.

The queen of Sheba, being a high priestess, was aware of the rituals of hieros gamos and was able to spend a lunar cycle with the king before returning to her homeland.

Once the queen of Sheba left, King Solomon became the legendary king who was renowned for his wisdom; as a result of the reunion he was initiated into the next quantum of his destiny. Relishing in the glory of their connection, King Solomon wrote his most famous poem The Song of Songs to the queen of Sheba. This poem is one of his hundreds of attempts to capture the essence of his eternal love for the other half of his soul.

Kundalini is a serpent-like energy coiled at the base of the spine. It is said to be a representation of the Goddess Shakti, who, together with Shiva, represents the twin flames in Hinduism – a story legendary for having created all that is with two protagonists, in a sort of big bang–inspired story from which all creation arose. As the story goes, Shakti fell in love with Lord Shiva and wanted to marry him, but he was hesitant about the proposal at first, as she still had to work on her spiritual development – this is similar to what twin flames do to bring positive changes within themselves before they can unite with each other and embark on a spiritual quest.

It is said that Lord Shiva has been meditating for thousands of years, as he is a representation of consciousness, while Shakti dances for him; she is the energy and power of Shiva. He waits for her to be absolutely clear that joining in infinite love is her true desire, and as their longing to be at one provokes his third eye to open, they dance together as the universe unfolds into creation.

In your light I learn how to love. In your beauty, how to make poems. You dance inside my chest where no-one sees you, but sometimes I do, and that sight becomes this art.

—Coleman B. (1997), The Essential Rumi

Twin flames meeting and kundalini awakening bring along many psychic experiences, such as past life memories, astral travel, awareness of chakras and auras, extrasensory perception, contact with spirit guides, dreams and visions and increased creativity and healing powers.

The power of three used in alchemy might be present, and you may be able to see it in each other, following the principles of the Three-Fold Flame. The foundation of the sacred union would involve uniting and merging love, power and wisdom through the heart and consciousness.

The pink plume of the flame represents love, the yellow plume represents wisdom, and the blue plume represents power or truth. Together these three frequencies create a perfect balance or, better yet, represent the triune nature of self-mastery. As for twin flames, they represent the sacred feminine, the masculine, and the oneness, or the third element, that is created between the two parts of the same soul.

The Three-Fold Flame is a beautiful representation of the divine spark that dwells within our heart chakras; you and your twin are two shining lights creating a third, two polarities fused together in oneness.

As the purpose of the twin flame union is to shift consciousness into the new earth, a new paradigm, the twin flame union, is fused by the kundalini fire, the power of God.

Twin flame separation sickness can be so painfully intense that you can't enjoy anything at that time, but it is the need of the hour.

The feeling of losing the connection can be terrifying, especially if you remember all the lives you lived with your twin. So to remember all that, feel all that love and connection and know you just came apart before the union is devastating. It feels like you're sky high, you see the Kingdom of Heaven and you've been given the keys to enter it, only for everything to be taken away from you and for you drop to the floor and hit rock bottom.

It's almost like you have to earn the right of passage to Heaven with your twin.

Twin flames require unconditional love; the awakened twin, or the twin who is aware of the connection and pursuing it will be awakened to true unconditional love.

And you really have to show unconditional love and integrity to navigate through these difficult situations; the soul is challenging you to expand beyond the boundaries of our society's belief systems.

Twins are not here to fit into society; twins are here to smash that social paradigm and shatter that template to show that there is a higher level of love, alchemy and connection, which is from the heart and the soul. So when you are in this situation, when you have coexisting contracts with other people, you will face the challenge as to what you are going to do about that, how you can navigate to union around that.

Everything can happen in a heartbeat, but it will not happen when you lie back and wait for it, when you obsess about it and try to force it, and it will also not happen while you're running around like a headless chicken.

So many are trapped by society's definitions of how they're supposed to act and what they are supposed to be, and this can feel lonely.

For twin flames this can be a key part of the mission they are here for, to break down the old definitions and perceptions of man, woman, relationship and love. Society often acts as if men are devoid of feelings and emotions.

Whether you are male or female, possess masculine or feminine energy, it's time to let go of any damaging old paradigms and patterns, to open up to new energies, new activations, patterns and a new era.

This relationship is more about doing inner work, achieving spiritual growth, embracing yourself, getting closer to your higher self and the divine, than it is about a hardcore romance between you and your twin soul. You might think you first have to unite and then start the twin flame mission, but I believe your mission task has already begun even before you've met, and in some cases, you need to pass various checkpoints before ignition and the eclipse. You know when union is close – when you are aware of your mission, you are very sure of it and are nearing its com-pletion. You experience the flipping energies, no more anger and resent-ment, now you feel calm, peaceful and, most importantly, balanced; you do not experience run-chase dynamics any more. You dare to take all the necessary steps to materialise the relationship from the spiritual realm in the physical realm.

Also, the steps to seeing an eclipse are supposed to be similar to the bubble-love phase you initially started with.

We all end where we start, or it can be seen the other way around: the endings become beginnings.

It's time probably to remember again that you are the one holding the key, that you are the master of your own destiny if you chose to take the reins and steer your life in the direction you desire if you chose to be aware.

To truly let go means to let go of your willingness to control time and expectations, to focus on your own self-healing and let nature take its course.

Once you plant a flower seed, you do not diligently watch it until it blooms; you surrender to mother nature and trust that it will be nourished daily so that one day when you return, you will witness the beauty of it blossoming.

In some cases, if one of the twins isn't as spiritually awakened as the other, this separation can serve as the perfect catalyst in their awakening.

We have to acknowledge that we are a walking universe, and you are the creator of your own reality. Many of us do great things, yet we are not able to follow our happiness because our society makes things difficult.

Above all, remember your uniqueness is your gift; your passions, your challenges, your personality are here for a reason. And so you and your twin flame together make up the unique code, DNA, that is required to reach union. Focusing on others and comparing their journey may just distract you from the path that your soul has been working to lead you the whole time.

If you don't work for your dream, someone else will get to work for theirs; in other words, if you don't stay aware of your intentions, it is easy to be pulled into someone else's version of reality. Unfortunately, if you read about other twin flames struggling with separation; on some level your mind is perceiving the fact that separation is natural to twin soul connections, that there are always problems and that your whole system is aligned with it and attracting it. If twins could realign with their own inner soul wisdom, uplift their frequency into love and disregard so much of what the experts and others have written or told them, there would be so much progress.

In the end, anything your mind has been revolving about this journey doesn't really matter – this is not essential to know for the bigger picture, because what we all what in the end is love. In the end, what we all want is to feel respected, loved, valued, be seen by the person we love, to be happy and share this happiness with the ones we love.

When you can crack open the shell of being merely a human, there is a wealth of resources that can be unhooked and harnessed for something far greater than merely existing. Once you surrender to the fundamental pull to come together, then you'll realise that you have just tapped into a tremendous force; like giant magnets whose power lies within their destiny to come together in the sacred union.

I have this deep knowing that the divine shall grant reunion when both the twins accomplish the mission they share; the key is to identify the mission you are assigned and work towards achieving it. Seek to know it if you haven't already.

You might begin to be focused on the idea that you want to do something great for the world; twins are meant for greatness, so this is all normal, and if your divine mission hasn't revealed itself yet, it will, so don't worry.

The following-the-crowd type of mentality will find us missing opportunities, either because we assumed things work out by magic or divine intervention, when, actually, we could have taken action to make the most of them, or because we presume it won't work out when actually it could.

The yang energy holder needs to be brave through the process, try to get in touch with the feelings in their heart regardless of physical circumstances and commitments because they have no greater responsibility than the one to their own soul and heart, to their own well-being.

Listen to the calling of your own heart and soul, try looking into yourself, not looking to the outside or the other twin to fix things. You have to face your own crap, do your own work and come into your own power and move forward that way. Do not wait, do not put your life on hold, waiting for years and years, because that is such a waste of life, and you aren't here for that.

Twin flames are here as messengers of light, pioneers of love, peaceful warriors of light and carriers of love; anything else is due to the purging process. Even twins who are stuck, hurt, running and chasing are here for love; they just don't remember it, or they are afraid to open up.

You two so truly believed firmly in your connection and your undying love for one another that you had no doubt that you would be able to awaken to your core aspect, your soul, your spiritual being, once you came to earth.

There is something peculiar about the twin flame relationship, but know that one fine day, you yourself will know for sure whether somebody is your other half or not; it'll all come naturally through living your journey.

You are two people who when you meet are less than whom you want to be, but together you become everything that you dreamt and more.

We shall not cease from exploration, and the end of all our exploring will be to arrive where we started and know the place for the first time.

—ELIOT T. S. (2001), FOUR QUARTETS

CHAPTER 21

The Eclipse

If we'd never met, I think I would have known my life wasn't complete. And I would have wandered the world in search of you, even if I didn't know whom I was looking for.

—Nicholas S. (2014), The Longest Ride

Once upon a time, one single soul split and found its place into two bodies.

I know that you've been brought up like every other person thinking God created us as perfect beings and that we don't need anyone else to feel loved and appreciated but ourselves. But if this really was the honest truth, then why are we so foolishly seeking for our other half, for our one and only, the person who was made for us?

If we were to believe ancient Greek mythology, we would know how uniting with one's twin flame even scares the gods.

Everything on this planet was created in pairs; why would it be any different for us humans?

It is part of a designed universe in pairs. The Pandora's box, the cradle where life began but also death, the plague that came as a companion to life. Nature is all about balance; all the world comes in pairs, yin and yang, right and wrong, man and woman, and what is pleasure without pain? We have 'one' person out there who is made solely for us, and that someone will make every other person before them look like a joke, and we have to go through this so that we do know when the right person enters our lives.

And when that happens, there are no more words left; you have said them all.

This is it, the kind of love you've always been seeking. They are your prince charming/princess who kissed you, and your entire life is transformed. There is no mistaking it – they are the 'one'.

Some people expect twin flames to be the ultimate fairy-tale love story, and in a way it is. It is a story that can end in love and happiness, a love that conquers all, but before that happens, there will be some unexpected twists and turns that make you wonder if this, in fact, is true love or your worst nightmare. This journey doesn't always take you on the fastest route to romance; this is not the primary purpose of this relationship though you have met your forever love here on earth.

Happily ever after doesn't mean perfectly ever after.

A happy ending is a fairy-tale concept; there is no such ending even in ideal romantic relationships. All relationships are growing, evolving all the time.

If you find yourself in those connections, you really have to be honest with yourself here and also the person you are in a relationship with as to how and whether you wish to navigate this.

There is the great divine timing involved here, so when you are brought in, it is always the right time to ignite, regardless of your physical circumstances. When you are brought up together, the soul kind of knows what it's doing.

Destiny does not abide by our schedule. Things happen when we aren't expecting them; things don't happen when we are assuming that they will. It's one of the great paradoxes of life, and this irony has a funny way of interfering in our life.

Despite the obstacles that life throws at us, despite the fact that twins usually meet under the strangest of circumstances – differences in culture, geography, caste or religion; belonging to the same gender; huge age difference; and cultural barriers – it is always important to acknowledge, and remember, that everything does happen according to its plan and its script.

A problem can exist when there is a blockage; the feelings want to let in, they are just outside the door knocking, but you are not able to let them inside. If you are seeking this feeling but are in an expecting mode, then you become dependent, and it will not work.

When you come in contact with your twin, it is like looking in the mirror; everything you've spent your life running from or denying is suddenly in front of you. What makes it so special is the life-changing and transforming process.

Without a doubt, there will be challenges and fears present, there will be phases of running and chasing, but regardless of any of these challenges, it is possible to unite and stay with your twin flame although it is speculated that this occurs only in one's last lifetime here on earth.

But somehow your souls always meet, and your passion always grows. Wherever you go, you can't seem to get the 'one' out of your mind; even when you attempt to go to new places where you have never been before, your twin flame is still there.

When the time comes, the universe will conspire in bringing you back together, and if they are the destined 'one', then there is no force that can stop you from uniting with them. Don't forget it's a matter of *when*, not *if*.

The universe works in mysterious ways; despite the intermittent separations, you must have stopped and wondered at one point how somehow you and your twin still stumble upon each other. I mean, how can it be just mere coincidence? Didn't it cross your mind that the universe is conspiring to bring you back together? That's why, no matter how hard you try, how many times you screw things up, the universe works behind your back and amends things on your behalf, and the universe always succeeds.

I think this is obvious, but it's still crucial to mention that you two aren't just in love with one other; you aren't just there for the security, appreciation, sex or love; both of you are there because you are like best friends who have grown up together. It gives the feeling that you two have been raised by the same parents or that you have lived the same life because you have the same interests, hobbies, same wants and needs. You are each other's biggest support and the biggest help in life; you are each other's teachers.

Think back to the person you were before you met your twin; you were entirely another person; you were doing a job that didn't bring joy into your life; you were chasing dreams that only turned out to be nightmares, but then your twin came, and nothing was the same ever since.

There aren't many in this world who are lucky enough to meet their twin flame in their lifetime. Sometimes, if they do, it happens while one or both are in a relationship, when being together is out of the question, but you still feel the passion within. You feel that something is pulling you to one another. Coming in contact with your twin flame might even hurt you because you have never felt this amount of love before. You will be staggered with the feeling of belonging, and your body, mind, soul and heart will be aching for them. Everything will pull you towards this person, and you won't even know why at that point.

'Out of sight out of mind' does not apply to the love and connection between twin flames. Twins cannot see and talk to each other for years, and their love for each other will only grow stronger.

You will love and cherish your twin flame, and it doesn't matter how chaotic it may seem at times. It's still about the desire between you two and those irrational emotions that you simply don't have an explanation for.

Despite years or even decades of no communication, despite all the hurt the relationship has caused, you will still tend to love that person for reasons you yourself can never comprehend or fathom.

It is most probably the love that has cemented you both in the spiritual realm for aeons, which you feel now in the physical realm, though pretty much nothing significant has happened between you both in physical reality.

No matter what happens, no matter how far you go from one another, in a perfect moment 'written in the stars', everything changes.

There is never, ever a wrong time for twin flames to come together because if it were, it wouldn't happen in the first place; they are always supposed to meet when they meet.

There is a lot of misunderstanding about what really happens in this final stage of the twin flame relationship. Some claim twin flames should get married, have children, grow old and live happily ever after.

No matter how nice that sounds in the books, this simply does not hold true in all connections; the final stage in this life may be a separation in your particular twin flame relationship.

Relationships usually get caught in an on-off cycle until both of you decide either that the relationship has served its purpose or that you should continue your 'happily ever after'.

When you decide once and for all, you are ready for this kind of love.

Often, a sure sign of the eclipse is that one of you will just know deep inside that the other is your twin flame; trusting your inner guidance is essential during any soul connection. It may not make sense on a mental level but can be sensed through the heart.

It's important to be clear that reunion is when you meet with the other half of your soul, to begin the twin flame journey in this lifetime. And union or oneness is the last and final stage, where the two twin flames come together as one. Uniting would need to be a mutual agreement to stay with or without marrying your twin flame. You just know; it's a feeling inside you.

Some people think twin flames are always in union or reunion, that this journey does not have to end in a union, or it is not even necessary to begin with.

Union means that you will reach a state of harmony with your twin, but it does not say you will agree on everything or that you will never have an argument with them again. You will be able to find your unique individuality within yourself, but together you will have a single purpose.

The direction in which your life will go, your values, your goals and desires will mesh perfectly.

The two halves of your soul finally resonate and are attuned in a state of union as close as can be in a relationship, while still being on the physical plane.

You will be free of the tumultuous nature of the other stages of the twin flame journey. So far it has been hard, with many obstacles thrown up to challenge your will and determination. All that remains in the final stage is your spiritual mission.

You may need to be just friends, though friendship can often be much more than a romantic relationship ever could be for some people.

Step out and realise how lucky you are that you have even met each other; not many people get that opportunity.

When you unite with your twin, it feels like you are surrendering a battle that has been fought inside of you, between the mind and the heart, the one which has been telling you that it's too good to be true.

The weight of the whole world has been lifted off your shoulders, your body, mind, heart and soul are surrendering to your faith, and it feels like liberation. This is the beauty of the twin flame journey.

When twin flames meet, they actually face their shadow selves in the shape and form of the person they share the most sacred soul connection with. Only when they finally come to terms with that fact and try to heal what they long denied will they understand that what they have been searching for all those years was unconditional love for themselves, starting from within.

But it took an external force, their twin, to help them reach self-actualisation. Because loving someone else, even with this earth-shattering kind of love, will not complete us, no matter how much we want it to. Even though a significant characteristic of twin flames is their unexplainable longing for their other half, it is not the other person who will make them feel complete. That desire will leave us full for a moment, but once our twin leaves, we will be left feeling empty. What is essential is giving ourselves that love first, recognising our own self-worth.

This consuming need on the part of people to seek for that person whom they know deep in their heart will provide the missing piece to their lives and bring meaning to their existence is, therefore, often misunderstood. What twin flame unconditional love really brings is something that already exists within, and what they are genuinely subconsciously looking for are parts of themselves that they must face but refuse to acknowledge.

For the eclipse to happen, we need to change our way of thinking. Bad habits, attitudes and outdated philosophies need to be wiped out. Within a short period, you will find yourself going through a rapid process of transformation, internally and externally, and your twin flame will live the same experience.

Union means that twin flames have made their journeys and are fully ascended; their soul has become one with the universe, its creator.

The twin flame odyssey is a designated journey to finding yourself; that's what this is all about. In the end, you will realise who you are, what you are about and what is your true meaning in this world, and every so often this journey will take you to new places, other countries or another continent, to begin a new life, the life you were born to live.

The reason for the union with your twin flame is to face your own unresolved issues and reach your highest potential so that you can shine light into the world. This physical union may or may not be part of the journey.

The union or oneness – in other words, the final stage of the twin flame relationship, the goal if you will – is full of mixed misunderstood messages.

The eclipse, usually the final stage, is reached when the runner stops running, and the chaser finally achieves their goal.

The truth is that no living soul has experienced the real, final stage of the twin flame relationship because it happens when we are no longer physical beings. It occurs when we ascend to a higher dimension of consciousness with our twin flame and join with them on the spiritual plane.

And that need not happen in this life or even the next. The twin flame journey in this life is but one part of a journey that you have been on since your soul was created, and will only end once the soul has been reabsorbed into the cosmos once more.

It's all a matter of perspective. The final stage in this life can take many forms, typified by the shared spiritual mission and mutual support in achieving spiritual goals.

But the actual final stage of the twin flame relationship is predestined and you, as the physical being that exists on this Earth, will know very little about it.

When you unite with your twin flame, both of you will become so fierce together that nothing that can stand in your way; you two can conquer the world with your joined powers. Everyone will envy you and wish they too had that someone whom they can take by the hand and show the world what true love looks like. Despite all the things you have been told before, to have someone that means the world to you isn't the end of the world.

You know you are in union with your twin flame when you can love and feel them without any barriers within you or when you get the same feeling you would get when she or he is with you or when there is no barrier to your feelings within you.

Words flow between you endlessly, your views so similar but yet different. When you are so much in love, there are no arguments, only debates.

They are the first person from you seek help too, the first you run to hear the good or the bad news, they help you get through all problems in your life, they are the ones that help you get the wisdom you couldn't have discovered by yourself. They are the first words you say when you wake up in the morning, and the last thought you have in your mind right before you go to bed.

When twin flames finally unite with one another, both of them will experience an acceleration of their spiritual growth and personal awakening.

They will contribute to your campaign, and you will find yourself achieving more together than you ever did when apart. We were blessed to experience the type of love most never find.

But union does not necessarily mean staying under one roof; it is much more than that.

Most of us spend a lifetime seeking for *that* something in our life that can help us feel whole and complete.

Both twins might be trying to find love outside themselves, instead of within.

But now that you've finally found what you're looking for for so long, you lose the urge to go out there again into the world trying to find *that* which will make you happy, because you are happy. And everyone around you can see that.

Of course, there will always be obstacles you two have to overcome, but you will always find your way back to each other.

We always read about separation, because that is when people seek answers to their questions. If you were in union, you wouldn't probably be here asking these questions and discussing things about twin flames.

If it's meant to be, your twin will eventually find you, when both of you realise there is a significant connection between you. And this just might move you to tears, mostly because it so strangely demonstrates the power of the universe, the power of love and the power of the human will. Because that's what gets you from there to here. The universe responds to your intentions, actions, mostly all your choices, your awareness, your transformation, your love.

We need to decide for ourselves who we really are and truly want to be in our lives, what are our core values and what we will tolerate or not tolerate, both in our own behaviour and in the conduct of others. Love can be many splendid things if we can learn to reflect it on others and do our best to find ways to share and express love in our actions, words and our thoughts so that we don't inflict unnecessary pain on others knowingly.

I believe that the twin flame journey is a test of faith in love because two souls who have experienced all their past pain, have complicated histories and a whole different life happening, suddenly start seeing and recognising themselves and cannot resist or stay away from each other.

We are all humans, and our past experiences may be rougher than others', our histories may be darker and even considered unacceptable, but this does not stop the twin flame experience from happening to any individual.

At some point, you might decide that you don't wish to wait anymore, that you deserve to be loved, and go and find yourself a new twin soul because clearly the person you are with now is not the 'one'.

The desire to find ideal love is often ego based; it can be fuelled by illusions or the need to feel special, be one of the chosen ones.

There is no guarantee that you will meet your twin, and if you don't you can still have a beautiful life that serves the multitudes; you don't need to be in a relationship with a twin flame to serve the world. Many spend years trying to find unconditional love, not even suspecting it is this twin flame love that will lead us to find it within ourselves.

It can take a long time to admit and accept they are the 'one', but that does not mean this connection is above any others; however, it's definitely noteworthy. You put them in your books, they put you in theirs. Now you're something; you're their special 'one.' And there will be days when you wish this had never happened, but you'll no longer ask yourself if they are the 'one.' Now you know that no one else ever will be, no one else ever can be the one, and if you come across another powerful connection, you won't be naive enough to think that maybe this is another twin or the real twin or anyone else like that.

Despite the type of romantic relationship you find yourself in, it will have to stand through difficult times and challenges. The main thing to remember from all these partnerships is that if someone is trying to move on, and it is vital that we let them go.

That's why in these kinds of relationships it becomes necessary at one point to get some time apart, to decide what you should do about the future, for growth and learning. Being together and apart from each other gives twins the ability to maintain balanced energy so that they can become one.

This is because, in spite of your attraction and deep connection, you first and foremost have to become as much yourself as possible. And that is when you will realise that the 'one' you are looking for is none other than you. That is when the sun and the moon will start moving, and the eclipse will start; that's how you will unite with your twin when you become the greatest and most authentic version of yourself.

And on your journey seeking for the 'one', in finding them, you realise you've found something even more important – yourself.

You were never really seeking for the 'one'; you were looking for that side of you that you know you can turn out to be when you are with the 'one', and that's the biggest lesson your twin flame will teach you.

This will get way beyond you and everything you thought about life and love; it will be magical, beautiful and most of all, it will be yours. Even if you decide it's too much, and you and your twin go your separate ways, there's no way you can deny that you two are parts of the same whole.

> *To see a World in a Grain of Sand*
> *And a Heaven in a Wild Flower*
> *Hold Infinity in the palm of your hand*
> *And Eternity in an hour.*
>
> —WILLIAM BLAKE (2019), SELECTED POEMS

Our twin souls always arrive when we are ready for them, not a second sooner.

If you are in a twin soul relationship, this is something that you will never question; you will never wonder if your twin soul is the 'one' or not because your soul will be content.

Not everyone will be united with their twin flame in this lifetime, but if it does happen, it has the chance to be that *once in a lifetime ain't nothing-ever-going-to-be-the-same* type of love.

Leaving aside the relationship you find yourself in, the love we are worthy of is also the love we deserve, which will want us as much we want it. The truth is, if you do love somebody, the only thing you can do is to set them free, knowing that if it's meant to be, they will come back to you.

And if they never come back, then it is just one of the most beautiful lessons we'll learn.

A twin flame always has to burn even on its own.

Only God could have designed this Love . . .

That vanquished every drop of resentment I had in me, the last and the first . . . because I feel reborn, I begin a new life, I start to exist, to feel . . .

I envisioned something . . . something similar but this is different because my imagination could not open the gates of Heaven, but today the gates of Haven have opened up for me.

Thank you, God, thank you for letting me live this love.

—Enrique Torres, Wild Angel

BIBLIOGRAPHY

Aaron B. Z. & Ruhama G. (2008). *In the Name of Love*. New York: Oxford University Press Ed., p. 39–136.

Dorschel A. (2002). *'Is Love Intertwined with Hatred?'* London: Journal of the British Society for Phenomenology Ed. , p. 86–128, vol. 41, No. 1

Esther P. (2017). *The State of Affairs*.London: Yellow Kite Ed., p. 213–321.

Gary B. (2018). *The Golden Ratio – The Divine Beauty of Mathematics*. New York: Race Point Publishing Ed., p. 105–127.

Lucinda E. C. (2013). *Walking Over Eggshells*. Umhlanga Umhlanga Press Ed., p. 278–307.

Puente S. & Cohen D. (2003). *'Jealousy and the Meaning (or Nonmeaning) of Violence'*. Personality and Social Psychology Bulletin Ed., Vol. Puente and Cohen, p. 60–76.

Robert H. (2015). *Divine Union: Decrees for a Heavenly Marriage*. Arizona: XP Publishing Ed., p. 33–45.

Renna S. (2007). *Math for Mystics*.Newburyport, MA: Red Wheel/Weiser Ed., p. 53–71.

Santata G. (2018). *Kundalini Exposed*. Santata: Real Yoga Ed., p. 78–96.

Yong K. C. (2017). Empty Your Cup. Yong Kung Chan Ed. Singapore, p. 95–112.

Zari L. B. (2013). When Love Is Lie. Vancouver: Post Hypnotic Press Inc Ed. , p. 67–89.

REFERENCES

Richard Hunter (2004). *Plato's Symposium.* Oxford: Oxford University Press Ed., p. 97–112.

William Shakespear (2013). *William Shakespeare's Poems and Quotes.* Ontario: Ink Walk Book Publishing Ed., p. 136–145.

Rabindranath Tagore (2005). *Selected Poems.* London: Penguins Books Ltd. Ed., p. 76–81.

Jalal Al Dim Rumi (2006). *Rumi: Poems.* London: Everyman's Library Ed., p. 233–245.

Johannes Kepler (2005). *Kepler's Astronomia Nova.* New Mexico: Green Lion Press Ed., p. 54–78.

Victoria Erickson (2017). *Edge Of Wonder. Ed.* Essex: New Leaf Distribution Ed., p. 43–96.

Emily Bronte (2015). *Wuthering Heights.* New York City: Sterling Ed., p. 245–327.

Martin Luthor King Jr. (1969). *Strength to Love.* New York City: Harper Collins Distribution Services Ed., p. 79–86.

William Shakespear (2008). *A Midsummer Night's Dream.* Oxford: OUP Oxford Ed., p. 25–45.

Albert Einstein (2013). The Ultimate Quotable Einstein. New Jersey: Princeton University Press Ed., p. 407.

Plato (2016). Symposium. California: Create Space Independent Publishing Platform Ed., p. 65–76.

Coleman Barks (1997). The Essential Rumi. New York City: Harper Collins Publishers Ed., p. 298–311.

Eliot Thomas Stern (2001). Four Quartets. London: Faber & Faber Ed., p. 35–37.

Nicholas Stern (2014). The Longest Ride. London: Sphere Ed., p. 378–398.

William Blake (2019). Selected Poems. Oxford: OUP Oxford Ed., p. 123–127.

Printed in Great Britain
by Amazon